The Greatest Networkers in the World

The Greatest Networkers in the World
John Milton Fogg

Book One | First Printing | 30,000

Printed in the United States of America

Published by The Greatest Networkers
A division of Success in Networking Press
2066 North Ocean BLVD #9 SW
Boca Raton, FL 33431

TheGreatestNetworkers.com

ISBN: 978-0-9833997-0-4

Library of Congress Control Number: 2011933154

BUSINESS & ECONOMICS / Marketing / Direct
SELF-HELP / Personal Growth / Success

Foreword

I once wrote a book...

The Greatest Networker in the World told the inspirational story of a young man on the brink of quitting Network Marketing, and the mentor who helped him turn his life around in one remarkable weekend.

Having sold more than a million copies, it's among the most well-known books in the Network Marketing business and many people have told me it has changed their lives.

Now I've written another...

Introduction

The Greatest Networker in the World was fiction. This book is different.

It's a collection of true stories of how twenty-one ordinary people came into Network Marketing and became successful—very successful... millionaires...

None of them had ever done Network Marketing before.

They knew nothing about the business—although some thought they did.

Many had reservations about it.

Most of them struggled—sooner or later.

Network Marketing transformed their lives.

And they all became millionaires.

Their clear message is:

"If we can do it, so can you."

This book is the best way I know to make people aware that an extraordinary life is possible through Network Marketing.

The diverse backgrounds, upbringing, education, life and work experiences of the people in this book show that Network Marketing is the most equal "equal opportunity" of all.

This business doesn't care about race, gender, age, education, past success or failure. Instead, what matters here is being open to learning, developing new skills, taking the inner and outer actions that generate success, and showing others how to do the same.

It offers the potential of personal fulfillment and extraordinary income for doing those things well.

This is a book about possibilities.

Yours.

Thanks for reading it.

I appreciate you.

More Than a Book

This is a relatively short book, 192 pages in all. If your flight is long enough, it's an "airplane read." There's a lot that's not in here that could be and probably should be.

There are no pictures and no bios for the 21 Greatest Networkers. Yet I'm guessing you'd like to know more about each of them. And most of them have written or recorded lots of material I know you'd find valuable and useful.

So, "More Than a Book" means there's a website that offers you all the things I could-not/chose-not to put in these pages. No strings, no charge; it's a rich resource for folks who are reading this book. It's here:

TheGreatestNetworkers.com/More

Table of Contents

Quit Quitting

Jordan Adler grew up in a 1,000 square foot home in a working-class neighborhood in the south suburbs of Chicago. His father was in the advertising business. His mom stayed home and took care of him and his two younger sisters.

Although Jordan didn't know any entrepreneurs growing up—though everyone in his neighborhood had jobs—he was always setting up lemonade stands and he had a paper route. He focused on giving his newspaper customers good service so he could be rewarded with bigger tips over the holidays.

Jordan became an athlete—gymnastics and track—primarily to have fun with his friends. What he did best in high school was party, and Jordan openly admits he did a lot of things that he probably shouldn't have been doing.

His dad saved up his entire life so that Jordan could to go to college, but with an annual income of only $28,000, at best, his father could only pay for one year of Jordan's education.

If Jordan wanted to finish college, he'd have to pay his own way.

Jordan went to the University of Illinois. He really wanted to go out of state, but that would have cost a lot more money. He had no idea what his major was going to be, but as soon as he got to college, Jordan met some guys that were "really cool" who showed him the Landscape Architecture Department. They were playing Frisbee in the courtyard and building bonfires at night. Jordan found his major.

He got a job as a night clerk, working from 11 PM to 7 AM and also worked as a resident advisor at the co-ed dorm. That's how he paid his way through school. Jordan worked very, very hard in all his classes for the first three years, because he wanted to take only electives—like gym, weight lifting and gymnastics—in his final year. And he did.

Right out of school, Jordan moved to Arizona with a suitcase, a guitar, and $250. He bought a little two-stroke Yamaha motorcycle to get around.

His first job was renting roller skates at a little place called Cheap Skate—it was the only job in his life that he'd ever be fired from. Jordan also worked at a fitness center as a salesperson. He did that for about a year. Finally, he got a couple of jobs in landscape architecture.

Jordan was always looking for ways to free himself from the 9-to-5 "rat race." He just didn't want to have to report to anybody. He'd read the classifieds to find opportunities and would go to these Network Marketing meetings and sign up with different companies with money he really didn't have. Literally, his "last pennies."

Jordan would get involved in a company, go to a couple of their meetings, tell two or three people about the opportunity and always get the same response: "No."

He figured there was something wrong either with the company or the product... or that he just couldn't do it and he would quit.

> **Jordan did that for 10 years with 11 different companies. But he was totally in love with the idea of Network Marketing.**

Back in 1984, Jordan had changed careers and was working for America West Airlines—a little start-up airline that had one plane and 179 employees. Jordan was #180. The airline was very entrepreneurial, but the pay was very, very low. People got stock options and $12,800 a year.

Jordan started off in customer service, but did a lot of different jobs. He was a flight attendant for a short time, worked in reservations, and even on the ramp! The airline grew to over 15,000 employees. It was an adventure for Jordan and lots of fun. But even though they were a phenom and became a household name, in 1992, they filed for bankruptcy.

Jordan was given a choice: He could either lay-off his people and stay for half the pay, or he could lose his job. His salary got cut from $28,000 to $14,000.

Jordan didn't have the confidence in himself that he could go out and find another job. He loved what he was doing, but it was getting pretty ugly. Still, he stuck around.

At that point, Jordan got involved with his 12th Network Marketing company. He had come to realize that regardless of the company he was with, he needed to personally sign up 20-30 people to find one who would go out and build a big business.

His thinking was:

> **"If I have a consistent plan to bring in one person a month for a couple of years, a few of them will really do something."**

There was a little place on Mill Avenue in Tempe, Arizona, called Coffee Plantation. Jordan would grab people he worked with at the airline and sit them down with a yellow legal pad and explain the concept of what the company was doing.

Jordan figured that if he did that three or four days a week, he could find one person a month who would join him. If he could do that for a couple of years, he would have sponsored 24 people. So that was his goal: One person a month. Jordan would show the business to three people a week on his lunches, Tuesday, Wednesday, and Thursday.

Jordan didn't have a personal success story when he started—and the company hadn't developed much in the way of marketing materials—so he'd simply tell people a little bit about his background and share with them why he loved Network Marketing so much. He focused on the value of residual income and having a check coming in whether he chose to go to work or not.

Jordan explained the product (telecom) and talked a little bit about what it did and how it would help people. He showed them the opportunity by drawing circles. He didn't have a strong upline, so there was nobody he could do three-way calls with. It was just Jordan—winging it.

As the company grew, there were more and more success stories and local events were held. Jordan would bring the interested people he'd shown the business to over lunch and they always sat in the front of the room. Even if he didn't know the speakers, Jordan acted like he did and he'd introduce them to his guests.

After doing that for three or four months, the top leaders got to know "that guy, Jordan Adler from Arizona, who was always bringing guests and introducing them."

If there were such a thing as a natural Networker, Jordan Adler was one.

After a few months, Jordan used his flight benefits to fly to an event in San Francisco. He was sitting in the hotel lobby and the top leaders in the company, Jay Smith and his wife, recognized Jordan and invited him to dinner. All the highest earners were there. At the time, they were all making about $10,000 a month. Most of them went on to make a quarter million a month. One of them went on to make over $12 million a year.

To Jordan, $10,000 a month was like winning the lottery. He didn't say much that night. He listened. And he thought, "I want to be part of this group, be their peer. I don't want to be just this guy in the audience who knows who they are. I want to be onstage with them."

At that point, Jordan—who today earns more than $2 million a year—had not yet sponsored one single distributor in his entire Network Marketing 10-year career!

But after that meeting, he went to work and started signing people up. He was just consistent with people, continued to follow up, continued introducing the business to new people.

Jordan went from believing to knowing.

"Most people," he says, "go in and out of believing and doubting, believing and doubting, but there's a point where you just know."

At that dinner, Jordan knew. There was no doubt. Sure he got discouraged, felt down, disappointments happened, but he knew he could do it. There was a future out there that would provide him with an amazing lifestyle. He also knew that in order to get that, he was going to have to completely run the course.

He quit quitting.

Jordan began selecting instead of selling. He stopped trying to turn a three of clubs into an ace. "There are four aces in the deck," he says, and his job was to find those aces.

He ended up enrolling 19 people in two years. From those individuals came a group of over 12,000 distributors and over 40,000 customers eventually making Jordan his first $1 million.

"The business is ridiculously simple," Jordan says. *"Ridiculously simple.* You put yourself in the flow of people, so you're constantly meeting them. You've got to get good at building relationships, connecting with people on a personal level. It's really just connecting and creating that level of trust between you and them, then learning how to call and invite them to take a look at what you're doing."

Networkers are always asking, "What do I say to someone to get an appointment with them?" For Jordan, they're asking the wrong question. He says you can pretty much say anything to someone you have a good relationship with. Focus on building that level of trust, then you can call them and say, "I want to show you something," and they'll say, "Sure, what have you got?"

What does Jordan believe it takes to be a million-dollar leader in this business?

"First," he says, "You've got to love people. Love people to the point that you're willing to let them be whoever they are, whether that means being part of your company or not, and continue to love them regardless."

It requires that you be on a journey of growth, both personally and financially. You need to be hungry. You need drive and ambition. "You've got to want more to a point that you're not willing to settle," he says. "You're just not willing to settle. That's just not an option."

"You've got to develop the skill of letting go and the skill of reframing."

"When I look at every single top leader in Network Marketing," Jordan says, "they're good at reframing things for themselves and for other people."

Every Networking company has people who struggle and every company has people who become wildly successful under the same set of circumstances. What's the difference?

Jordan says, "It's people's ability to reframe and their ability to let go of those tough situations, because everyone has them." There's not one successful leader he knows who hasn't had to deal with tough things on their journey. It's how quickly you can let go of those difficulties and re-focus on your future.

As cliché as it sounds—and Jordan is sensitive to using clichés—the best thing about Network Marketing, for him, is the freedom. It's the ability for Jordan to call his own shots.

"I travel a lot," he says. "I've got residences in multiple places. I choose to spend time with the people who I really love and care about. This business gives me the opportunity to contribute and really grow. There's never ever a week that doesn't pose some challenge and the opportunity to work through it. Usually, your life is pretty fulfilling when you're constantly growing."

"At the age of 52," Jordan says. "I can still go after my dreams, continue to live a higher quality life and bring other people along with me."

"It just doesn't get any better."

It's Who You Become

Margie Aliprandi was so embarrassed by all the presents she got for Christmas, she would hide them away before her friends came over. Her young parents were lovingly devoted to her, and they gave Margie everything she ever needed and wanted. It was a good thing.

She was "spoiled ripe."

Margie was a very happy child.

But one thing her mother and father couldn't give her was a confident, out-going personality. Margie was very shy.

When Margie was eight years old, her dad gave her a reel-to-reel tape recording of Russell Cromwell's personal growth and development classic "Acres of Diamonds." She listened to it for hours on end. And she fell in love with the idea of being the best you can be—with becoming a diamond.

In the eighth-grade Margie gathered the courage to try out for cheerleading. Her mother pushed and Margie's own motivation pulled. She made it. That effort set a pattern of achievement she would repeat throughout her life.

Margie blossomed in high school, maturing into a warm, loving and outgoing person. "Still not overly confident," she says, "still not in my full stride, but pretty grounded and with a strong sense of purpose."

Margie went to Brigham Young University for a year before transferring to the University of Utah. She was deeply involved in music and drama.

Straight out of college, Margie became a junior high school music teacher.

Margie married and had her first child, Shaun, two weeks before school started. She would run over to nurse him on her lunch break. Three months into that first year of teaching, Margie was pregnant with her second, Nicole.

Margie loved teaching. She loved the music, the kids. She did *not* love the routine or anybody telling her what to do. On her first day back after Christmas vacation, she dropped Shaun off with his grandma and cried all the way to school, sobbing, "I don't want to do this anymore."

Margie quit teaching after that first year, had her second child and a couple of years later, there was a third, Todd. During that time she was doing some acting; spokesperson work in television commercials. It was good money—way more than she made teaching. It wasn't consistent, but it was a great supplemental income for a stay-at-home mom.

Margie had been married seven-plus years when she decided it was the right time to move on. It was a difficult decision and a difficult time for her: Single mom, three little kids, not wanting to lose the home she'd moved into recently. Margie reluctantly signed a contract to go back to teaching music.

A few weeks before school started, Margie met the company where she would become a multi-millionaire. But first, Margie would need to overcome one minor challenge: She *hated* the idea of Network Marketing.

"My whole adult life people had been hitting me up about Network Marketing," Margie said. "They'd tell me, 'Oh, my gosh, you'd be perfect at this,' and 'You're custom made for this business.'" Margie's dad was involved with an MLM company and he knew that with her drive and vivacious personality Margie could be a star in the business. But when he invited her to join him, her reply was...

> **"I'd rather clean toilets for a living. I'll never do Network Marketing!"**

What changed?

One of the spokesperson jobs Margie had done was for a nail-gel system that gave women beautiful salon quality nails in the comfort of their home for a fraction of the price. She'd done all their promotional videos, used the product herself and loved it. The company was a fledgling networking enterprise with 13 or 14 products doing about $28,000 in monthly sales, but the founders knew the nail system was a knock-it-out-of-the-park product and they wanted Margie involved.

> **"If there ever was anything I could sell, this would be it."**

She canceled her teaching contract and jumped in with both feet. There was nobody to teach Margie what to do, but she did enough things right and her business began to grow.

"I remember my very first meeting," Margie says. "I invited a bunch of people. Four came. Two joined. Right away I thought, 'Ratios. I get it. You know; four people come, two people join. I'm going to double my efforts.'"

The next week she invited twice as many people, but no one came. So, Margie went to a movie. But the message was clear and loud: Results came from action. Want greater results—take greater actions.

She did trade shows. She talked to everyone; anybody who crossed her path. Margie would talk to the woman handing the food out the drive-through window, ask about what she was doing for her nails. "You've really got to see this product," she'd say.

Things started growing very nicely—and no, Margie did not take off like a rocket. There were plenty of tough times.

Margie couldn't afford plane tickets, so she drove everywhere the business was taking her; from Utah to Louisville, Kentucky (1,583 miles) with 10 nail systems in the back of her Subaru wagon. And she went regularly to do meetings in California.

Margie couldn't afford to stay in hotels, so she'd stop in a well-lit parking lot, sleep in the car, wake up and drive to a gas station. She'd put in her electric curlers in the rest room, throw on a dress, some makeup, and go off to her meeting where she'd tell her prospects, "Hey, join me! We're going to make a million bucks."

Then exponential growth started to kick in. The massive action paid off. Margie had created some real momentum.

Margie had the vision that every single home in America was going to own one of her nail systems, and she and her team would be the ones selling it to them. Her business was based on volume. "You get 10 of these and you get three other people to get 10, you're an executive and you're making this much money." The product was the vehicle, but the financial opportunity was driving the business.

Within a year, working exhaustively, Margie was making more money in one month than she could have made in an entire year teaching school. Two and a-half years later, at age 35, Margie had made her first million dollars.

When Margie gets firmly fixed on a goal, that's all she sees. She also has the ability to help other people do that for themselves.

Margie Aliprandi

There's simply no "quit" in her. Never has been.

Her first business trip to New York was a disaster. The taxi driver got lost and she arrived more than a half hour late to the meeting. The handful of people who hadn't left the stifling hotel room ranged from irritated to hostile. (Remember, these were New Yorkers.) Margie cut her three-quarters-of-an-hour presentation into minutes and just wanted desperately to be done and away ASAP.

She ended the meeting with a politeness she didn't really feel and invited people to stay and speak with her if they wanted. Only one man did—a short, bearded, violin-maker from Connecticut with a thick Russian accent. He told her he had seen "the big picture" and was going to take the business to Russia.

It was all Margie could do to force a smile, pat him on the shoulder and say, "You do that... Good luck." Then she got out of there as quickly as she could.

Within a few months, Margie began noticing Russian names on her downline report. Then more and more Svetlanas, Olgas, Irinas, Igors and Pisarevskys kept showing up. At the high point of her growth, Margie had more than 500,000 Russians in her organization. From that dreadful meeting in New York, Margie had sponsored a nation!

Margie's resilience and persistence, combined with her love and caring for people—and her willingness to do anything to help them be successful—proved to be the perfect preparation for Network Marketing leadership.

In her 21 years—all with one company—Margie's had her way ups and far downs. There were times when some former corporate leaders behaved very badly indeed. But she always saw the corporation itself as a company of destiny: They had the right product, the right plan and the right mission.

When she had her fourth child, Ashley, Margie stepped back, determined this time—for the first time—that she wasn't going to miss a moment of her child's "tiny years." Besides, she was exhausted. She'd endured all she could from the former founders of the company at that time, and although Margie loved them like family, it was time to pull away.

In those two years that Margie was "semi-retired," her residual income never fell below $15,000 per month. Margie eventually came back into the business, but she uncharacteristically had her doubts. She wondered if she had the emotional stamina; the passion it would take.

Margie figured that if she could just help everybody that was making a $1,000 make $2,000, everyone that was making $5,000 make $10,000, just help them double their income, then she'd double hers. Within the year, Margie had done just that.

One thing Margie says...

> **"It's easy to get into Network Marketing. The real question is, 'What's it going to take to get Network Marketing into you?'"**

"You build your belief in yourself, in your company, in your products or services that you offer, and in Network Marketing," Margie says. "You grow that belief until it's abundant, inviting, and just bubbling up out of you and you become a natural magnet to people."

And Margie knows that belief requires proper perspective. Success rarely happens over-night. For the most part, you'll want to give your business good, solid, massive action, and you've got to plan to do that for a few years. She urges people not to reinvent the wheel. Margie says it's crazy when there are tried and true systems and tools in place. Just *use them.*

Margie loves the money, and the freedom, that success in this business brings. She can't imagine working for somebody else. Margie loves being able to do what she wants when she wants.

The lifestyle Network Marketing has afforded Margie and the amazing upbringing she's given her children really are beyond her wildest dreams. And the richness of the relationships and partnerships her business has brought her are incredibly valuable.

"I've been a part of helping people change their lives dramatically with both their health and wealth," Margie says, "I've helped to do that all over the world. My 'why' now is to do what I do, knowing what I know, in order to help people in the North American market with the same desires to become millionaires."

For Margie, what's most valuable about Network Marketing is...

> **"Who you become in the process, and who you help other people become."**

"All the vacations that my kids and I went on, the house, the cars, they're all great, but that's not going to matter in 100 years. What really matters is the growth. It's knowing that even if you were to lose it all today, inside you know that you created something great from scratch, and you called on yourself to do it, and you didn't let yourself down."

For Margie Aliprandi, knowing *that,* then helping other people develop that same knowing, is the most valuable thing of all. Margie found her "Acres of Diamonds" in Network Marketing

---

Living My Best Life

Lynn Allen-Johnson's world turned upside down when she was 16. That's when her father and "best friend" died of Hodgkin's disease—leaving behind her mom and six kids. Lynn's family was devastated. They quickly fell apart and went their separate ways.

By the time she was 19, Lynn was married, soon had two children and was divorced five years later. Out on her own, with no education and no money, it took Lynn all she had to survive and raise her kids. She lived on government assistance and food stamps. She worked two jobs; sometimes three.

Lynn freely admits her kids didn't get the best from her. Far from it. They spent most of their childhood in daycare—and although that's still a painful thought, Lynn knows now that she did her very best to be a great mom and provide for them.

> **"I didn't have a lot of belief in myself, but I am a survivor. I knew I was going to take care of my two daughters no matter what!"**

Today, after more than 30 years of struggling just to survive, Lynn is in a very different space.

"I'm very, very blessed," she says. "I didn't come from a great place, but I'm in a great place now. All I lived through helps me to empathize, to understand where people are coming from. Because I've been poor—I know what it's like not to have. Now, I know what it's like to have in abundance."

At the age of 50, Network Marketing gave Lynn Allen-Johnson that first chance she never had.

At that time, Lynn was working 60+ hours a week and just grateful that she had enough money to pay her rent. She'd moved "up" to a three-bedroom apartment in Florida, which was the nicest place she'd ever lived. Although Lynn was constantly broke, she felt like she had finally arrived... somewhere. At least it was somewhere better than before.

But Lynn was struggling. She was working way too hard. She was putting in longer and longer hours and doing her best to cope with the stress of a job serving wealthy customers who were as far from broke as could be. As a result, she was having some health challenges and she was worried about herself.

Lynn's daughter sent her some nutritional products she hoped would help. Lynn felt better quickly. She began experiencing, "an amazing sense of well-being." Her health and vitality continued to improve and her worries vanished.

And others noticed the change.

"People would tell me, 'Lynn, you look amazing. What are you doing?' and I'd say, 'Well, I got these products in the mail.' And they'd say, 'How do I get them?' I'd say, 'Well, I really don't know much about it, but maybe you'd better call my daughter because that's where I got them.'"

Lynn had no idea what was happening.

Her daughter told her, "You know, Mom, you're going to tell everybody about this. That's who you are. You're going to share this and you might as well become a distributor."

Lynn's reaction was immediate and harshly negative.

"This is one of those pyramid things. I'm not going to do *that!*"

Lynn's daughter patiently explained that it was just word of mouth marketing—person-to-person advertising. Since she was going to do that anyway, why not sign up and just share the products with people?

That's how it began. Lynn was in the business. People called her to get products. She started getting a couple of paychecks.

"Oh my gosh! I'm getting a paycheck every single week in addition to my job!"

Lynn felt like she'd died and gone to heaven, but it took four-and-a-half years before she *really* understood what she'd fallen into, before she was willing to make a commitment to the business. Lynn was simply too caught up in what "everybody else might think" about what she was doing.

Like most people, Lynn didn't want to be rejected, so she avoided approaching people about her business. She asked herself, "Why would these people listen to me? I'm a nobody." Finally, Lynn realized that she was the only one asking that.

What changed was Lynn's attending her company's International Convention. She actually went to prove to herself that *she couldn't succeed.* Instead of the turn-off of three-piece suits and slick sales types she expected, Lynn found people just like herself: Real, ordinary people who were living extraordinary lives. And Lynn knew for absolute certain...

"If they can do it, I can do it."

Lynn used that pivotal event to decide that this was going to be the way she was going to create freedom and have control of her life, for the very first time in her life.

Once Lynn got it, her train started moving *fast* and people could hop on or get out of her way. She was no longer embarrassed about the business. She started learning more about Network Marketing and quickly understood that this was the best route for most people to have time and money freedom. And she *owned* that. It was *real.*

No more, "Gee, I have a product that can help you." It was "I have a business that can change your life."

When it became a real business for her, Lynn knew that she just needed to select a few people. She began using an interview process where she would tell people, "In two years this is where I'm going to be. I am selecting a couple of partners. Let's sit down. See where you are. This may be for you and it may not. Let's just look at it together and see."

Even though she hadn't gotten anywhere yet, Lynn's presence and posture were so different that people began to follow her.

Her vision was so strong people wanted what she had even before she'd gotten it herself.

It was a total change in her. Lynn had taken ownership of her future.

Lynn reasoned that she just needed to find four key people. There were 18 million people in Florida and she thought, "How hard can it be to find four?"

She saw her job was to spot them, help them get everything they wanted from this business and take them to the top. And that's what she did. The whole thing happened with a shift between Lynn's ears.

What were the skills Lynn developed and practiced that created her success?

First and foremost, she says, she became a good listener. And that was new for Lynn. In the beginning all she did was talk.

"I was always dumping all over people. 'Oh my gosh, you guys, you've got to hear this... yada, yada, yada.' Once I committed to listening, I started by sharing where I was going, then asked, 'Tell me about you: What do you do? How's your family?' Every meeting I had, I listened for probably 80% of it. Then I would say, 'I have something that might help you get there,' and I would show them what they were going to have in this business."

Lynn wanted to get inside of people and find out what they wanted, what they needed. Because...

> **Unless they were hungry, unless they were committed to their success, Lynn knew that we weren't going to go anywhere.**

She looked for people who had a huge need, a big desire, and a commitment to do whatever it took; with failure not an option. "Don't tell me you'll give this a shot for six months. I want to know where you want to be in two years." Then Lynn would put a plan together to get there... together.

Lynn never really worked hard at finding new people. She met them as she went about her life—at church, in the mall. Lynn knew her mission and she only wanted certain people.

Wherever she was, Lynn always kept her eyes open. She listened. She looked for people with good hearts. People who wanted more in their lives.

"I attracted people who are a lot like me," Lynn said. "People who realize that we have to get over ourselves, we have to get a strong belief. Once we have that, we have to figure out a way to help other people achieve greatness. All of it comes back to us."

It was all about establishing a relationship. Then, if it felt right, she'd say, "Hey, I have something I'd like to share with you that I think would be mutually beneficial. Give me your number and I'll call you and let's have a cup of coffee next week."

Lynn always looks for people who see the value in helping others and who understand the concept that *when you give, you receive*.

"One of the most powerful things about Network Marketing for me is that I can be who I am. I can be a caretaker, I can want to make a difference, but in order for me to get paid, I've got to help other people. That's basically what I'm about and so this was perfect for me."

"I'm looking for people who have the heart to make a difference, people with integrity, and people who want more." She found them. Lots of them.

"Those are the three things that I sought after in people," Lynn says, "and more often than not they found me. I didn't have to go out and look hard for them, because I attracted them. I just had to know they were there by keeping my mind on my mission and listening to who they were, because that's how I decided who I was going to pick. That's still how I decide who I'm going to choose to work with today."

Lynn has been one of the top 10 worldwide income earners for years in her company. She is a Network Marketing millionaire. She "retired" her husband years ago and in 2008, Lynn took 15 members of her immediate family—all of her grandkids, her cousins and her mother—on a Caribbean cruise. She paid, and had "the most amazing, amazing time."

The best thing about Network Marketing for Lynn is that it's allowed her to live "my best life."

"No education. Nothing." Lynn said. "I started in my mid-50s from a place of being dead-broke and never having done anything like this before. Where else does somebody like me get the opportunity to live this type of a life? It just doesn't happen anywhere but in Network Marketing."

"I wish everybody would get that each one of us can have this if we just open our minds to what's possible. Get rid of the negative ideas and realize we have to take responsibility for our future."

"The best way to predict the future is to create it."

"You can choose what you want to have, who you want to be, where you want to go, how much money you want to make through Network Marketing," Lynn says.

"You can layout your own blueprint and design your life by choice, not by chance."

"That's what I did and every day I'm just so grateful."

Chicken or Champion

Richard Brooke grew up on a 3,000 cattle ranch in what is commonly known today as the San Joaquin Valley. His father was a Stanford graduate. His mother was a Mills College graduate. "It was an isolated growing up," Richard said. "Most of my relationships were with animals, either pets or wildlife. The nearest neighbor was two miles away."

Richard didn't socialize with the other kids very much. After school he had a long trek home, and once home, he had ranch chores to do. (Back then mothers didn't chauffeur their kids all over the place.) The only activity he ever participated in was Cub Scouts. At the beginning of sixth grade, Richard's parents sold the ranch and moved to Merced, California.

After high school, Richard was a fireman for seven or eight months. He really loved that. He was a search and rescue diver and an engineer on the truck. Richard thought he'd found his vocation, but budget cut-backs ended that career.

Richard then went to work at Foster Farms, the largest chicken processing plant in the world. His job was to cut up chickens as they sped by on the production line.

Richard did that for about six months and got so good at it they let him teach other people how to do it.

Four years later he was running a department of about 300 chicken cutters, responsible for human resources, hiring, firing, negotiating with the union, training and staffing that department.

Richard's vision was to work there for the next 36 years, retire and be able to fish and hunt and hang out at the local bar like all the other retired chicken plant guys. But the company had a policy—more than a glass ceiling, it was a *steel* ceiling—and he couldn't advance any further in management unless he had a four-year degree.

Richard didn't have a degree, no time in college at all. He hated high school and the last thing he wanted to do was go to college.

One of Richard's best friends, Steve, who had gotten him his job, called him at the plant one day and said, "Hey Brooke, you got to come to this meeting tonight; got an opportunity to make a lot of money."

Steve was sort of a bold, brash, arrogant, kind of person and that call didn't sit very well with Richard, who told him, "I'm not interested." He didn't hang up on him. He just brushed him off. A short time later, Steve called back and said, "Brooke, you're out," and he hung up. Richard just laughed and didn't think anything of it.

Richard was 22 years old at the time. He can't even remember using or having a distinction for the word "opportunity."

He never had any financial guidance at all, and his friend Steve was one of the least credible people he knew when it came to work and money.

A few weeks later, some people who worked for Richard at the chicken plant came and asked him for time off to go to a meeting in LA, which was about five hours away. Richard asked, "What kind of meeting?"

They said, "Well, you know, Steve... the financial opportunity. We're getting involved in this thing. We're going to make a lot of money." That both irritated the heck out of Richard—and it got his attention.

A couple of weeks later, Richard just happened to be driving close to Steve's house. He thought, "I'll just stop by and see what's going on with Mr. Financial Opportunity."

Richard walked in and there was Steve, sitting in the middle of his living room in a pink three-piece polyester suit (it was 1977), four or five people around him, also friends of Richard's, and he had a very expensive cold-cut platter they were all digging into on the coffee table. Steve was celebrating his first commission check from the company. It was $1,834.18.

Four months later, Richard learned that the check was for rebates on Steve's personal purchase of $10,000 worth of fuel additive he bought through his Network Marketing company, so that he would reach the *supervisor* position and could then go to a seminar that was for supervisors only. The $10,000 came from Steve's mother—an inheritance that had been set aside for Steve's college.

"So if it weren't for the front-loading of $10,000 worth of product and the $1,834 check," Richard said. "I don't know if he would've ever got my attention, but he did. After the little party, he took me back into his bedroom. We sat on his waterbed. He took out a yellow pad and started drawing circles: Five of you, five of you, five… until I was blind. That was it."

All of his friends were involved and Richard couldn't stand the thought of any of them breaking out of that town, making $10,000 a month and leaving him behind.

"Really, I wasn't motivated by gain for myself," Richard said. "I was motivated by not wanting to get left behind. And it wasn't that I didn't want them to have it. I was all for them having it. I just wasn't for them having it and me *not* having it. That would amplify my deep-rooted feelings that I 'wasn't enough' to begin with, although I didn't know that at the time."

Richard describes his beginnings in the business as "horrible."

"I was an introvert," he said. "I did not like people very much. I didn't like salespeople. I'd never heard of Network Marketing; Multi-Level Marketing. I had heard: 'Ding-dong, Avon calling.' That was the extent of my direct sales awareness."

"Every time I thought about myself doing the business," he says, "selling the product, recruiting people, the mantra that just came back from deep within was, 'I can't do this. Nobody will listen to me. I don't know anybody who'll want to do this.'"

"One day, after three weeks' worth of meetings and looking at the 'Five of you, five of you, five...' it occurred to me that the way I was going to make a lot of money doing this was not based on what I did, and not based on what the people I would recruit did. If I were going to get rich, it was going to be coming from the third, fourth and fifth level down, from people I didn't even know."

The light switch came on and Richard just said to himself, "Wow! I can do this!"

"I just started recruiting," Richard said. "Trying to recruit anybody and everybody including the guy who ran the chicken plant. He told me, 'You know, really, you should probably go full-time. Let me pack up your office so you can get prospecting and out of the plant.' I think I was fired. All I remember is sitting in his office trying to recruit him and the next day I was full-time in Network Marketing."

Richard's 1099 his first year was $12,000. His second year was also $12,000. His third year fell to $4,000. In his fourth year he earned $100,000. His fifth year was right at $400,000.

"Somewhere in that third year I just started doing what I was telling everybody else to do," Richard said. And he made an inspired decision in what he calls a "chicken-or-champion" Y in the road. Richard's version of what some people call a "defining moment."

"I believe your success in this business is made up of hundreds and hundreds of seemingly insignificant opportunities that are just little Ys in the road. If you take the left bend in the road, you go back to the chicken plant. If you take the right bend, you go on to be a champion."

"It's much easier to take the left, because it's just easy," he said. "It's tougher to take the right, because that takes vision and courage and motivation and faith and all that stuff."

"I had a retail customer call me for more product," Richard said. "He lived three hours away. This was in the dead of winter in Iowa and it was in the middle of an ice storm."

"I didn't have any business driving anywhere," he says. "The roads were a sheet of ice. But I thought, 'If I drive three hours in this ice storm, this guy's going to be impressed. And if I time it right, he'll buy me lunch.' Which was a critical strategic move because I didn't have money for lunch?"

"I believe as a result of doing what I now call vision and self-motivation work that I was naturally led to an inspired decision, an inspired conversation of possibility. 'If I drive three hours, he'll buy me lunch. If I drive that far, I can sell him a case. If I sell him a case, it's $185. I'm rich! I can go a month on $185.'"

So Richard hopped in his car and drove to the Village Inn, in Cedar Rapids, Iowa. Jerry Shaub met him there. He was very grateful Richard drove all the way to deliver him product. He asked Richard about case prices. Richard told him.

"He said, 'I'll take a case.' He says, 'How about lunch?' Ha! Perfect," Richard said. "We're having lunch. He's asking me about me and what's going on and everything, and he says, 'So, is there any money in this?'"

"I looked him right in the eye and said, 'It'll blow your mind.' My gross income at that point was somewhere around $300 a month."

"I could've looked down at my paper," Richard says. "I could've stuttered, I could've stammered. But I looked him right in the eye and I said, 'It'll blow your mind.'"

"Jerry loved it. He says, 'I can do this.' I thought, 'Wow, you can.' Finally I found somebody who can do it. And he said it in a way that I believed him, too. He really meant it."

"Then he says, 'Okay, what's next?' This was a Thursday, on Saturday in Kansas City, which is about a five-to-seven-hour drive away, the president was having a big meeting. I not only told Jerry he needed to be there, I told him he needed to have guests there."

"It would've been so easy for me to say, 'Well, there's a meeting in a couple days, but that's too short a notice. I'm sure you got other things going on. It's too far to go.' But I made an inspired decision. These aren't things you think about; they just come out of your mouth if you're motivated."

Jerry made Richard $100,000, practically all of his income in his fourth year. Three years later Richard was making $40,000 a month and had 30,000 people in his organization doing about $2.5 million a year. He was 26 years old.

Richard went on to find three more Jerry Shaubs soon after, "Because," he says, "then it was easy."

"When you are inspired, when you're motivated, you just naturally talk yourself into opportunities," Richard says. "And if you talk yourself into enough of them, they're going to lead to extraordinary things."

"Every aspect of personal development is tested in Network Marketing, because this is a people-intensive business," Richard says. "It's the people who make the difference, and it's the difference that you make for other people that makes the difference in your business."

"And," he adds, "there just isn't any other economic business vehicle where a person can get started like I did for a few hundred or a thousand dollars, begin on a part-time basis and three or four years later, have a net worth in the millions because of their residual income."

"I just love the personal development and the wealth-building attributes of Network Marketing. There's nothing else like it in our society and economy today. Nothing."

The Gift of Network Marketing

Art Burleigh grew up in Birmingham, Michigan, 16 miles north of Detroit, in a middle-class, suburban environment. Art says he was blessed to have both his parents throughout his whole life. His dad is still alive—almost 93—and his mom passed on about 11 years ago. Art had a brother, Keith, three years younger than he was. They went to public school together. They were in Cub Scouts and Boy Scouts together, too. Keith died of a heart attack when he was only 35. Art misses him greatly.

If there is such a thing as a born entrepreneur, Art is one.

He had a paper route from the sixth through the 12th grade. He was responsible for delivering the *Detroit News* every day; rain or shine or snow or sleet, or worse—and there were times when it was worse.

Art had a lot of customers and serviced them well. He really did a great job and got lots of nice Christmas tips. Art always felt he was pretty wealthy, because he didn't have any expenses: No phone bill or heating bill or car payment or anything. All the money was his. In his junior year of high school, he invested that money in a trip to Europe with a group of Explorer Scouts. They toured Europe for six weeks. "Travel really opens your eyes," Art says.

"Travel is not a luxury. It's homework for a meaningful life."

"I've always enjoyed traveling," Art says. "Not only for the fun experiences that I've had, but the perspective on life that it gives you." It's been Art's life-long passion.

After high school, Art went to the University of Michigan in Ann Arbor. He joined a fraternity and majored in speech and theater.

After college, Art went to California and a through his growing network of connections got a job in the Mailroom at Universal Studios. He had no aspirations of being an actor. Art liked the technical, producing side of theater and musical theater best. He went to law school at night and eventually worked his way up to the legal department and performed a lot of contract analysis and copyright work. Then he got a job over at United Artists in Hollywood, putting together movie distribution production deals as a business affairs executive.

Remember "Heaven's Gate"? The 1980 movie was a way over-budget ($44 million) box-office bomb ($3 million), and it crushed the studio. Art's boss was out of a job and so was he. Through a friend (networking again) Art shifted over to a marketing career where he worked successfully for the next dozen years.

In 1988, a friend, through a neighbor, introduced Art to Network Marketing. "I was pretty fascinated with it," Art says. He was with a water filter company, for four or five years, but never really made the kind of money he had hoped to.

"I was new. I didn't have great training. I was doing it part-time. Maybe I missed the growth curve of the company," Art said. "Who knows? But it was very educational."

Art learned about relationshipping, about sales, about promotion, about recommending and about word-of-mouth marketing.

It was his first experience with a business model where you could build a team and generate an ongoing stream of mailbox money from residual income.

Art knew all about royalties from Universal. He'd done contracts for directors, movie, producers and production companies, and he knew what kind of residual income was built into all those deals. Art wanted a piece of that, too, but until Network Marketing, he had no idea how to get it. And now, he knew.

He explored several companies during the early '90s, was with some for only a few months; others longer. One particular company really looked to Art like it was going to fly, but closed right out from under him.

It was a crushing experience for Art. "We'd worked really hard," he said. "Got things going. We had a good group and it seemed like we had a lot of momentum. But their product was overpriced and it wasn't consumable. I didn't understand all these nuances then, like how important consumability is and correct pricing for the market. So, that one didn't fly."

But all those experiences introduced Art to more people, and the relationships and friendships he formed led him to the company he would stay with for 14 years.

One of those friends sent Art a fax about a new company that was being launched, with some little stories, some testimonials. More faxes kept coming and finally Art read them to his wife Marlyn in bed one night. He said, "If these stories are true, I think we could have a lot of fun building a business with this company. This is a very beneficial product." So that was the start of Art's career with the company that he had the most fun with so far.

Art and Marlyn sponsored 12 people in the first two months. Eight of them went to sleep and four of them went to work.

From that group of four they grew an organization of 150,000 around the world.

"It only takes a few people to really catch the vision," Art says. "They went to work with us, and we connected with people that they knew and we brought on some others in the course of the first few months. We kept prospecting, so did a handful of others and that grew the team.

"I think there's always an element of luck in the building of any large Network Marketing organization," Art said. "We were lucky to find a lot of distributors who were looking for a new home, because the company that they'd been with was deteriorating and they wanted something better. Some of the people I didn't know knew them and attracted them to our group. That really caused huge growth."

Art was an Eagle Scout when he was in high school, so he learned leadership at a young age. In college, when there were meetings at the fraternity house, Art noticed that when he spoke, people listened. And he thinks that's because first, he listened to them. Art had the ability to listen pretty thoroughly to all sides before he put in his two cents.

Leadership and listening are skills that have served Art extremely well in Network Marketing.

Art also had a lot of training in reading detailed documents through his law background. At the movie studio, he had to write what's called "digests of contracts," which are two-page summaries of 85-page contracts. So he was able to summarize complex things like the pay plan and create the kinds of support materials the company and his group needed.

Through his years of experience in marketing, Art also knew that stories were very important, because "Facts tell, but stories sell." "Testimonials were starting to come along about our products," Art said, "so I collected them, put snappy little headlines on a whole bunch of them, and published them in an eight or nine-page set. We kept getting those fed out to our organization either by snail mail or by fax."

Art always tried to keep nourishing the leaders on his team with the best support resources he could find or create, whether they were books he recommended or articles or summaries of the pay plan, or business or product success stories.

Most people in Network Marketing are part-time. Art knew the best way to stimulate production, cooperation and excitement with a volunteer army like that was to nurture people's imaginations, their hearts and their dreams—to feed their hope that they can really succeed at this.

"People need to have resources that build their belief in the company, the products, in Network Marketing and in themselves," Art says. "So any and all of those things that I could find that helped with that, I passed along."

And Art listened to his team's concerns and passed those concerns along to the company.. He was the Chairman of the Executive Advisory Council, a group of leaders that kept the company and the field connected and in communication.

After 14 years, Art's company abruptly went out of business. The recession, some bad financing strategies and other factors behind the scenes that Art had no control over destroyed the company. Suddenly one day, the commissions just stopped flowing.

"It's very depressing and discouraging," Art said, "because we worked so hard for so many years to build a great team, and we poured our heart and soul into it. We hoped it would live for a long, long time."

"We sort of knew it was coming," he said. "We just didn't know when. So we had plans to make a shift, but starting over is starting over. It takes time to rebuild an organization and restore the trust and belief system of our team members who will stay with us and want to come over to something new."

One mark of a true Network Marketing leader is not simply building a big organization once, but doing it again.

And Art Burleigh is doing it again—and it's going great!

Art believes that what it will take to recreate his former success is focus, perseverance, communicating honestly and openly, and a willingness to take responsibility for being the harbinger of hope for dozens and hundreds and thousands of people.

Art has always tried to do what's best for the people on his team, even when it didn't seem to be in his own personal, immediate best interests. "Because long-term," he says, "if we're honest and open and supportive of the people on our team... Well, I think what goes around comes around."

Give to get. That's important to Art. "I think the law of the harvest is a major factor in how we succeed," he says. "Because we've got to do a lot of planting and nurturing of seeds in order to expect a harvest. And we really never know where that harvest will come from. If we behave in integrity and with consistent smart actions, the harvest, I think, is bound to come."

After a few years in the business, Art learned that the people who really grow your team, and who ultimately become most important in the success of your organization, are almost always people you don't know in the beginning. That was certainly true for him. The people Art brought on board initially lead him to the leaders that really grew his organization, and created the most growth for the team—and the most income for everyone involved.

As he sees it, Art's "job" is to help people achieve their dreams.

Art Burleigh

"We give people hope to get where they want to go in life and then we help them get there."

Art thinks the time freedom and the financial freedom are the most important things that Network Marketing provides. "It's life-changing," he says. "And, I should add the personal development is life-changing as well. It improves our awareness of what it takes to become and be a better person."

"And," he adds, "Network Marketing allows parents to stay home, to spend a lot more time with their kids. There are so many single parents and latchkey kids who aren't able to spend time with their parents. It's really important for parents to be there with their children, so that their kids have great relationships with them and learn more from them."

"That really was a blessing for our family—the time we got to spend with our son Seth. Being with him. Being there for him. At soccer practice, taking him to school and back, the wonderful vacations we took together as a family."

"That's the real gift. That's the gift of Network Marketing."

I Am Network Marketing

Eddy Chai was born in Kuching, East Malaysia, known to Westerners as Borneo. Kuching is tropical rain forest, the wettest populated area in Malaysia with an average of 247 rainy days per year.

"I come from a very, very good family," Eddy said. "My father was a government servant and pretty high up. He is the Chief Superintendent of the City Hall of Kuching."

Eddy has one brother and three sisters and he's the youngest. When asked if his siblings picked on him, Eddy replies with laughter, "Oh, no, no, no, no! Everybody spoiled me."

He was an average student, but he did well in all his important exams and as a result finished "Upper Six," the equivalent of the 13th grade—something very few students achieved in Kuching at the time. That pretty much guaranteed Eddy a senior government servant post. As a result Eddy joined the Police as a Direct Inspector and went to a special unit, the Police Field Force, who specialized in jungle warfare, much like America's Green Berets or Army Rangers.

Eddy spent five years fighting the Malaysian communists.

A good friend of Eddy's father—the Head of the Chamber of Commerce for Malaysia and one of the richest men in the country at the time—encouraged Eddy to go into business and gave him the money to get started. So Eddy left the police force and began building restaurants, cafes and grocery stores. And he did well.

"My sisters had immigrated to Canada," Eddie said. "They were telling me all the good things about living there and the opportunities there and they actually applied for me to migrate. It was so easy, they applied for me and before I know it, I got a letter asking me to go for medical check-up and my application to immigrate is approved. So, I left home and went to Vancouver."

"I was excited, you know. When you are born in a small, little town in a very backward country like East Malaysia, you have the desire to go see the West."

"When my greatest opportunity came up, I just packed my bags, sold all of my businesses and left for Canada."

When Eddy arrived in Vancouver, all his friends and relatives kept asking if he was interested in starting a Malaysian restaurant. But Eddy told them, "We should not try and change the taste and eating culture of the people here. We should open restaurants selling food that Canadians eat." And that meant hamburgers.

One day, Eddy drove around town, saw a small restaurant by the beach, sat down and opened the menu. It had quite a few hamburgers. "Now you must understand," he said, "a guy from Malaysia, 30 years ago, does not know what is a hamburger." So, Eddy ordered them all.

"The waitress asked me, 'What in the world are you doing?' I said, 'Well, you know I want to learn how to make hamburgers.' She laughed and went back to the kitchen. The owner came out and he said, 'Sir, I've never seen... if you want to learn how to make hamburgers, there's an easier way. Come to my kitchen tomorrow and, I'll teach you how to make hamburgers.' After a month, I bought a place and started my own restaurant."

And Eddy did great. All his restaurants in Canada were very successful. He also went into real estate. As a restaurant owner working 16, 18 hours a day, you have no time to spend money, so whenever he accumulated enough Eddy bought property, six properties in all. He was on top of the world.

"But you know," Eddy says, "in business, you can be successful 10 times, but you cannot fail once."

Eddy failed in just one business, the White Rock Public Market. He lost everything.

But just before he lost it all, Eddy had joined a Network Marketing company.

Eddy owned the only café in the Ocean Park Mall, a place where he says even if you didn't know anything about the restaurant business; you could still make money, because there was no competition. One night a customer, Calvin Carr, approached him and asked Eddy if he was interested in making money. He said, "Sure, everybody is." And Eddy made an appointment to speak with Calvin after he closed shop that evening. He thought they would be talking about real estate.

Eddy made coffee and they sat down. "Calvin told me he was going to tell me about the greatest opportunity in the world... Network Marketing. I lost my smile and nearly took back the coffee!"

"If he had told me upfront that it was Network Marketing," Eddy said "I would never have given him a chance. I knew all about MLM. My neighbor and several of my customers were involved, and one of my sisters and her husband were, too. I'd even refused to listen to a presentation from them when they wanted to show me the business."

Eddy told Cal, "I'm not interested and besides, I have no time." Calvin replied, "Eddy, I'm already here. Will you give me one hour?" Now as a Chinese man, culturally, Eddy really couldn't say "no" to his request, especially since he invited Cal to come and tell him about this money making opportunity. So Eddy told him, "Okay, but hurry up about it." Eddy was doing pretty well for himself at the time and thought the very idea of "selling soap door-to-door" was beneath him.

That one-hour turned into four and when Eddy got home that night he couldn't sleep.

At around 4:30am, he drove back to his restaurant and collected all of his customer's business cards that he'd kept and started making his prospect list.

The following Monday, Eddy jokingly told his customers he was going to sell his restaurant and go into another business. A real estate agent by the name of Scotty was in the restaurant and asked if Eddy would let him sell the place. He said he'd do it in one week. Two hours later, Scotty phoned back and told Eddy he'd already sold the place—to himself!

Eddy met with Cal on Tuesday, and told him he'd sold his restaurant and was going to go full-time right away. Cal explained that the company was opening in Taiwan that November, and asked if Eddy if he would like to go there to do the business.

Eddy had never been to Taiwan, didn't know anyone there and didn't speak the language. Cal told him, "Don't worry, you are Chinese, like the Taiwanese, and everyone in Taiwan speaks English."

That September Eddy arrived in Taiwan with his family and got down to work immediately. He quickly learned everyone *did* indeed speak at least three words of English. "No speak English."

In spite of the challenges and language difficulties—and being newly bankrupt—Eddy went on to become one of the company's biggest distributors. When he left after six years, his organization accounted for one-third of their business in Taiwan with over 100,000 distributors.

Eddy spent a year as one of the highest paid consultants for Network Marketing in Taiwan and Southeast Asia. It was while in this position he found his next company where he worked over 20 years and built an organization of more than 2 million distributors in 25 countries around the world.

How did he do that? Eddy says simply...

"Work like crazy."

"If you want to be successful in Networking or any business," Eddy said, "we should remember the teaching by Jim Rohn—Work six days a week, half a day. To be successful, we cannot work the time of normal people."

"You know," Eddy continued, "Many people work eight hours a day, five days a week. To be successful, we have to work half a day. Doesn't matter which half, the earlier half or the later half. Doesn't matter which half. Learn to work 12 hours a day, six days a week, all the time."

"Not for one week, or one month, or one year. No, no, no. *All the time.*"

"I've been working like this since I started business; six days a week, half a day, for the last 30-40 years," Eddy said. "It's the Law of the seeds. You reap what you sow. If you sow sparingly, you also reap sparingly. So, sow... like crazy."

And just what seeds do you sow to create the phenomenal success Eddy Chai has achieved?

"All distributors should decide which they want to be," Eddy said: "A follower. A leader. An outstanding leader. Many people are not successful because they are just followers. Many people are only a little bit successful because they are just leaders. If you're talking about great success, a leader has to decide that he's going to be an outstanding leader."

As Eddy teaches: An outstanding leader has vision—a belief in *why* you want to do the journey. "Everything starts with desire, dreams, vision," he says. The second thing is unwavering courage. And third is that an outstanding leader must be knowledgeable.

"One of the things I insist on in my training," Eddy says, "is my leaders must teach the right answers."

"They should not teach on how they feel, or what they think. What they think and what they feel may be the wrong answer. They should not also think from their heart, because if they do that, sometimes you get a heart attack. Of course learning is just the start. Then, we have now to put that knowledge to work."

"There is a very common saying in English, okay, 'Knowledge is power.' Knowledge is not power. Knowledge is only power that can be put into action. So, get knowledge and get to work. One of the most common mistakes of Networkers is they spend so much time thinking and not enough time doing."

"I'm a pretty strong Christian," Eddy said, "and in our faith there are many things the Bible teaches us what we can do and what we cannot do. How we should think and how we should not think. What we should say and what we shouldn't say. A lot of people ask me, 'Eddy, how do you become a great Networker?' I give them this poem I wrote:"

> I asked God to give me a big organization and God said, "No." He said He gives courage and it is up to me to build it.

> I asked God to give me knowledge to build this organization and God said, "No." He said He gives wisdom and it is up to me to learn.
>
> I asked God to take away my pride so that I will learn and God said, "No." He said it was not for him to take away, but for me to give it up.
>
> I asked God to give me happiness and God said, "No." He said He gives blessings, but happiness is up to me.
>
> I asked God to make my spirit grow and God said, "No." He said I must grow on my own, but He gave me a 'Book' to guide me.
>
> I asked God to help me love my associates as much as He loves me. And God said, "Ah, finally you understand Network Marketing."

"When I was doing Networking at the very, very start," Eddy said, "you must remember, I lost my business in Canada. So, my goal of course, was to make money. I became a millionaire very, very quickly. But very soon, Network Marketing became more than just money. It became a way of life—travel, recognition, power and influence, working with my wife, an example for my children. It became part of who I am."

> **"Network Marketing is my life. It's me. I am Network Marketing."**

"I thoroughly enjoy it."

The Defining Moment

Ken Dunn was born and raised in Halifax, Nova Scotia. His dad was a career officer in the Canadian Navy who had enlisted when he was 17, served time in Korea and then in both parts of the Gulf War. Ken's dad would be away serving at sea for most of the year.

Ken has learned to be a very positive guy, so he says things like "he didn't really have the finer things in life as a kid" and that "he wasn't born with a silver spoon." But if you push him on the subject you'll learn he was poor and he hated it. That's important, because it's been a driving force for Ken his entire adult life.

Tired of hand-me-downs and beat up shoes when he was a young teenager, Ken created what he called the "Exchange Program." He'd walk into the department store wearing his worn out sneakers, try on a brand new pair of Converse high tops, walk around a bit to make sure they fit, then he'd walk out the door leaving his old pair behind under the chair.

Once after doing an "exchange," he was stopped by security. Ken was ushered into the guard's office, ordered to sit down, and the officer told him that he'd been watching Ken and he knew he had stolen some watches. The guard called Ken's father.

Ken's father, being both a naval officer and a dad, was none too pleased that his son was accused of being a thief. But it became clear pretty quickly that Ken didn't steal any watches, and he and his dad left the store—Ken wearing his new "exchanged" sneakers.

In his high school yearbook, some friends wrote under Ken's picture:

"Most likely to end up in jail."

And he did, but not the way you may think.

At a job fair in his senior year of high school, Ken spoke with a recruiter from the Halifax police. He was very interested, but the officer told Ken to come back in a couple of years. He had to be 21. Right next to the police was a booth for the Canadian armed forces. The recruiter had overheard Ken's conversation and asked, "Would you think about the military police?" Ken would. He enlisted. That was the beginning of a 15-year long career in law enforcement.

Ken was a detective. He investigated murders, robberies, drug trafficking and worked on a variety of SWAT (Special Weapons And Tactics) teams performing high-risk operations that fell outside the abilities of regular officers. Ken was good at his job and enjoyed police work, and he learned a number of skills that would serve him well over the years.

Having to testify thousands of times in court honed Ken's organizational skills and taught him to be top-notch communicator. He also sharpened his instincts and intuition and became a quick and perceptive judge of people.

Ken developed laser focus, determination and a bias for action.

All good things. But there were other qualities that were not so good.

Police detectives have to be in control at all times. Their own lives and other people's lives depend on it. And Ken became pretty strong in that department. Seeing all that pain, suffering and death so often, and so close-up left Ken jaded—not without compassion, but hardened. He was compelled by his work to become manipulative and dominating. And it follows, that he also developed quite an ego.

Finally, after 15 years of policing, Ken's son was born and he wanted out. He started looking to find something that he could do to really have the type of life he wanted for himself and his family.

While still on the force, he got involved in a number of business ventures on the side—from importing silver Mexican jewelry to mortgage financing. Ken started three different enterprises from scratch and all part-time. Each one became a million-dollar business. Ken clearly had "The Touch."

Ken's involvement with Network Marketing began with his best mortgage client and friend, John, a real estate man who consistently sent Ken $80,000 of referral business a month. He asked Ken to take a look, but Ken didn't really need to. He said, "Sure," and signed up right away, even though he had a no-to-low opinion of Network Marketing.

Given Ken's drive and skills, it's no surprise he took off like a rocket. He made $2,400 his first month, and $10,000 his fourth month.

By Christmas of that year, Ken was at $25,000 in monthly earnings. That's when the roof caved in.

He worked hard and built fast. It was really amazing to watch. But remember those "not so good" qualities Ken had developed along with his strengths? They finally came round full-circle.

On Christmas Eve, Ken's two top leaders arrived at his door, presumably, Ken thought, bearing gifts. But that was not their intention. They'd come to tell Ken they were quitting. Why? They couldn't take it anymore and the "it" was Ken. He was, they told him, a manipulative, dictatorial, controlaholic and they were fed up with him alienating their people. And $25,000 became $2000 in less than two weeks. Ken's Networking organization was dead.

Ken did not "take it like a man." The tough cop shut himself in his office and cried. He honestly didn't have a clue what to do. But he did know one thing: He had to change. Fast. Starting right now. Or Network Marketing was over for him. True to his nature, that's what he did.

Ken threw himself into his reinvention with the same drive and passion he does most things. Though it was unfamiliar territory, he dug in, drilled down, and, by studying the "Inspirational World Leaders" he admired most, Ken began a concerted effort to adopt their best qualities of character and make them his own.

Ken Dunn could build a business blind-folded with one hand tied behind his back, sound asleep. His personal reinvention took more effort.

Ken realized all those folks in his group were gone and he was going to have to recruit all new people, so he did. He sponsored 10 new people in that first month and then doubled that. About six months later his income was already back up to $10,000. Ken learned a valuable lesson.

"Each and every one of us is going to go through tough stuff. We're going to have days we just want to give up," Ken says. "I realized that whatever happens to you is day/date stamped. It's in the past. The person you sign up the next day has no idea that your business went sideways, that your company didn't ship its product on time, that a bunch of people got slowed down and off track because some commission checks were late, or whatever the situation was."

"When you go to bed at night, the day is done," Ken said. "So leave all the negative things behind. Don't even mention them. Those new people that come into your life that next day and onwards, they'll never know about it unless you tell them. And why would you?"

What makes Ken a Greatest Networker? First and foremost, he's never stopped trying to get better at prospecting—never stopped recruiting. Even today, he's always constantly trying to get better.

What Ken knows for a fact is that in terms of recruiting and prospecting, people only join the business because...

"They know you, like you, and trust you. "

"Unfortunately," Ken says, "most people make an opinion of another person within the first five minutes of an interaction. So, you always have to be working on having the best first impression you can. That includes your physical fitness, your health and wellness, your mental clarity, and your ability to connect with people and create rapport." So Ken studies those things like a science.

What does it take to be a million-dollar annual income earner? By now you know Ken's not going to candy-coat his answer for you.

"Listen," he said. "I've excelled at the highest levels in Network Marketing. I've traveled in 40 countries. I've had over 300,000 people in my downlines and made millions of dollars."

"What I know is that it is unadulterated hard work."

"What's been a fortunate experience for me," Ken says, "is that I've had success in three other businesses outside of Network

Marketing. The farther along the road I've gotten in this business, the more I realize that it is absolutely no different than success in any business. There's not one single person on this planet that started at ground zero and built significance in any industry who will tell you it was easy."

"It takes a lot of work," Ken says. "Real blood, sweat, and tears. It takes guts and determination. It takes a real laser sharp focus on you developing the best you that you can be. And that is *not* just lip service. That's the truth."

"There's this real consciousness on creating the right image for those around you to aspire to be like," Ken says, "because you're the example. You're the leader. That takes internal work, developing the right ideals, the right values, the right goals. And that stuff's not easy."

And on top of that, as Ken points out, it's about never giving up or backing off.

"The top leaders in the world are the hardest workers."

"You've got to build it up before you can sit back and enjoy it," Ken says. "It's to the victor comes the spoils. That's the guy who has won the war. Until then, it's a dogfight. You've got to put the effort in, the work in, the time in. You've got to be willing to sacrifice, and there's no easy way around that."

And the pay-off is...

"Network Marketing is a profession unlike any other on the planet," Ken says. "It grabs you where you're at and throws you into a place where you end up growing. It's a cliché, but the biggest thing for me about Network Marketing is it's helped me to grow, to become who I want to be. And it was through one of the biggest adversities in my life."

"It's funny, I spent 15 years in murders, homicides and death, yet I'm saying the biggest adversity in my life was when a couple guys quit the Networking business and gave up on me."

"Working through that really was my defining moment. That's when I realized that I needed to grow as a leader, and it's where I fell in love with the study of leadership."

"The size of my bonus checks, the growth and retention of my group, is directly related to the growing I do as an individual."

That's really what Network Marketing is for Ken: An unlimited income stream where the money you make is directly proportional to the amount you grow. And it's become his life passion.

Making a Significant Difference

Sandy Elsberg was born in Brooklyn. Then the family moved to a city project in the Bronx where Sandy, her sister Stacey and brother Brad grew up.

Sandy's father was a trucker. He drove 18 wheels for 60 years of his life. Her mother was a checkout person at a supermarket. "I had great love, had a great life," she says. "We were never shallow on hugs and kisses and food on the table. Times weren't easy. A lot of times they were pretty tough."

At least once a month, Sandy would dip into her babysitting money and peel off one-dollar bills to give her father so he could put gas in his truck. "He always paid it back with interest," she said.

"The three of us had a beautiful childhood," Sandy remembers. "There was no sibling rivalry. No fighting. Just had a house full of love. Money was an issue, but it didn't affect our being together."

Sandy moved back to Brooklyn, graduated from high school, went to Queens College, got a BA in education, and then went on to get her Master's Degree. She became a first grade schoolteacher in one of the worst schools in the city of New York: Ocean Hill Brownsville, Brooklyn. It was the '60s, around the time of the Vietnam War, and being on the "front lines of change" was important to Sandy.

"I always wanted to make my living by making a difference, and do well by doing good."

That was Sandy's motto and it became the theme of her life. For Sandy it was always about inspiration and making a difference in the world. It was about being significant.

"And it was about giving a life to these children," Sandy says, "and having them step into the world of possibility, knowing that there isn't anything that they can't do."

Sandy took that on and she took it on huge. She was that rare committed, creative teacher most parents pray for, but rarely find.

At the beginning of the school year, Sandy had each of her children bring in an empty juice can. They spent a day going through old magazines and cutting out as many eyes as they could find. Then they pasted the eyes to the outside of the cans, and Sandy filled each can with beans and sealed it. She called them "eye cans."

Every time a student had trouble with a problem, the whole class would shake their cans to encourage and support. And when the problem was finally solved, and it always was, the cans shook even louder to congratulate. Sandy always believed in her kids, and she made sure that they knew they could do anything they set their minds to.

Sandy taught school there for 10 years. Her kids performed over the city average and she loved every minute of it.

In her next life, Sandy became a holistic practitioner. That's where she met and married her husband, Bill. She practiced deep tissue massage, neuromuscular massage and colon health. She took that career on the same way she took on teaching. The same way she takes on everything.

Bill introduced her to Network Marketing. He always laughed and said, "I created a Frankenstein."

They were living in Phoenix, Arizona at the time. Bill came home one night and said, "Get dressed up. We're going to a hotel." Since they shared a health facility and a home with another couple,

Sandy thought, "Oh, private time. Yippee!" She put on her high heels, low-cut dress, and Bill took her to... a business opportunity meeting for a company selling aloe vera products.

There were 300 people in the room. The man in front was wearing gum-soled shoes and plaid polyester pants, and he was clapping. He went, "Hi everybody!" and clapped his hands. Then he said, "It's going to be a really great night!" and he'd clap his hands again. Sandy was looking over at Bill thinking, "What are you doing to me? I hate you."

Sandy had other ideas for the evening, but by the time the night was over, she was mesmerized by the testimonies and people who were doing well by doing good. It was stimulating. It was exciting. Yet she just couldn't wrap her head around it. Couldn't believe it. She thought, "This has to be a Brooklyn bridge thing, you know?"

Bill told her, "I really want to do this with you," and Sandy said, "Well, I'll tell you what, I'm really not interested. I came out here to build a clinic. I'm not going to support you in this," and Bill said, "Come on. What would it take for you to be supportive?" Sandy said, "Well, if you can get to a thousand dollars a month in six months…" That was their overhead. Sandy figured that would be impressive. Wait and see.

Bill was gone every day, every night. He would leave the clinic early, come home late. Sandy's father kept calling and saying, "Where's Bill? He's never home." And when her dad would call Sandy would say, "Well, he's out doing this Network Marketing thing." Her father said, "Well, how much is he making?"

When the first check came it was $111, Sandy's father said, "Follow him, baby. He's got a girlfriend."

The next month, the check was $300. The following month it was $500 or $600. In 90 days, Bill spent about $3,000 investing in the business and was not even making $1,000. Sandy's thinking was, "Okay, what's wrong with this picture?"

Bill said to her, "You told me I would have six months." The next month the check was over $1,000, then over $3,000, then over $7,000.

By the time it hit $3,000, Sandy was licking stamps and saying, "Can I take a letter, honey?" and "You need to write a manual for this," and "How can I be of assistance?" Sandy was finally and fully on board.

It started little and it went really big really quickly. They were successful enough that Sandy and Bill went away on a trip through the Grand Canyon.

When they left, their check was around $7,000 and Sandy knew it was going to drop because it was summer in Phoenix—100 days of 100+ degrees—and they'd be gone for almost a month.

When they got back and Sandy first looked at the check, she thought it was $1,100. Her heart sank. "Boy, that's really a big drop," she said with real disappointment in her voice. "It'll be like starting all over again."

But Bill said, "Come here and take a look at this," and Sandy said, "Yeah, what about it? We'll build it back up." She was trying to be positive. Bill said, *"Look closely."* It wasn't $1,100. It was $11,000.

They'd created momentum. "That's where you've duplicated yourself so many times that people can go on without you," Sandy says. "Now you can just get out of the way, sit in the back row and not have to be in the front of the room. And what comes after momentum? Pandemonium."

Sandy has experienced that same wild ride a number of times in her 27-plus year Network Marketing career. After her initial success, she experienced an equal degree of failure. She walked away from the industry a couple of times. But she always comes back.

"I don't quit," Sandy says. "That was the first thing. I didn't quit."

"There was a lot of falling down," she says, "but I never stayed down. And I didn't look to the right or the left. I just ran the race—like Secretariat. And no matter what the disappointment, I always had positive expectancy. I saw myself already being there on top."

"Even though I was driving a beat-up Volkswagen camper van with no heat, no air conditioner or radio cassette deck. $250,000 in debt. Putting back the large bag of diapers to get the small, for crying out loud, just to put milk, butter, eggs and bread on the breakfast table... Oh when you remember those days," she said. "But I never lost sight of the goal."

Sometimes there is fortune in misfortune: Sandy's been in different Network Marketing companies eight times in her career. She worked to the top of each one. Some left her and other's she left for greener pastures. Not the green of money or envy. Integrity issues were more often than not literally the heart of the matter.

Leaders are like that. And Sandy Elsberg is a leader of leaders. "Leadership moves me from the seat of my soul," Sandy said. "Leadership is about purpose and principles. When you're leading and coming from the God within, everybody gets it."

"They know your heart," she says. "They know your goodness. They get through your New York brazenness and the Brooklyn accent. And they get to a place where they love you and they trust you and they know that you're in this every step of the way with them."

"I think leadership is about respect and about treating everybody equally, because you never know when the sad, tired and broke woman driving the beat-up car is going to be the next leader of your company."

"Respect, treating everybody equally, coming from the God within, and that's love, isn't it? I think love is what leadership is all about." Sandy says, "MLM means Make Love More."

For Sandy, Network Marketing is the means to getting to your life's purpose.

"It's about getting what you can from life and being the possibility of your own existence," She said. "I think that Network Marketing is a vehicle to create a great life and to show what a great life can be like."

"Once you get past the grind and the grunt of working in a place of just being alive and functioning and biting your nails until they bleed because of the bills... Once you get to that place of being financially independent," she says, "you can then give to the world in ways that you've never dreamed of before."

"Network Marketing is about the transformation of lives and communities. It's about building significant relationships. For me it's about connectivity, it's about being on purpose to connect with people," Sandy said.

"I mean, people have done amazing things in this business. Look at the lives of the leaders in our industry who are doing big things in the world. You'll see proof that Network Marketing truly is a vehicle you climb on and drive away and make a difference."

"Network Marketing is all about creating a tipping point where the momentum changes people's lives so they become unstoppable."

"Network Marketing isn't the end; it's the beginning," Sandy says. "The beginning of making your life count and being the king and queen of your world. The royalties given in Network Marketing allow you live your life's definite major purpose."

"It's not, 'What can I get from life?' It's, 'What can I give to life?' What are my gifts? What are the strengths that make me unique and how do I play with them full on? How do I do that? How do I get out of the stands and onto the field?"

Sandy's answer is Network Marketing.

When Bill Gates, who dropped out of Harvard to do his thing, spoke at their Commencement he said, "I hope you'll judge yourselves not on your professional accomplishments alone, but how well you have addressed the world's deepest inequities." Sandy thinks that's what Network Marketing does for people. It is a way to help the world connect and raise its consciousness. She believes that at the end of the day it's all about love, being kind and it's all about doing good.

"There's a huge change coming," Sandy says, "and I think Network Marketing is allowing a lot of people to move forward in ways they could never have gotten to without the ability that this industry gives people to go from a *residual income* into *retirement* and *respectability* and then on to a state of *rejoicing* where they can *recreate* the planet."

For Sandy Elsberg, that's making a difference and that's significance.

All You Got Is Enough

Randy Gage came from a small family; a single mother who raised three kids by herself, back in the day knocking on doors selling Avon products. And Randy really does mean his mom went out and knocked on doors, literally.

Randy's mother worked very hard and loved them all, and did her best to set a good example. She had character and a strong work ethic. They were poor. That presented challenges. And Randy never knew his father, but as he says, "My mother raised us good."

As for school... Randy hated it.

He didn't fit in at all. He was pathologically shy and very insecure. He became a teenage alcoholic and drug addict. He skipped school, got suspended a lot, and finally was expelled before he was 16.

If you asked Randy what saved his life, he'll tell you it was because he was a reader. He was always reading something. Sometimes, he'd read a book a day. It's a passion he continues to the present time.

Randy recently got his GED (General Educational Development: a group of five subject tests which, when passed, certify that the taker has American or Canadian high school-level academic skills.), so he could take some college courses, which he has: French and Spanish, humanities and political science. He has no interest in getting a degree. Just wants to challenge his thinking and continue to grow.

Since college was not an option, Randy went to work. His first job was a dishwasher at a restaurant working for minimum wage. It was the only job he could get. He worked his way up to cook, waiter, host, and finally to a manager trainee, then assistant manager and eventually he made restaurant manager. "Which," he says, "is every dishwasher's dream."

Of course when he became the manager Randy realized that it wasn't the American dream—it was the American nightmare. He was working more hours and making less money than he made as a waiter.

Obviously, he thought, the secret is to own your own restaurant. Be your own boss. So, Randy and his assistant manager scraped together some money and leased a restaurant. That was "an unmitigated disaster." They ended up giving it back to the guy who had leased it to them and Randy went back in the business of managing.

Fortunately, along the way Randy had discovered Network Marketing and he made a little bit of money with it. He was working 14-15 hours a day in the restaurant, which left little time to do anything else, but he pursued both paths.

His first big check from Network Marketing was $11,000. That plus some money he'd saved up was enough to take on a new partner and try again with another restaurant.

As Randy says, "I was a slow learner."

He started a pizza place that was open until 4:00 in the morning. He'd go in at noon, work all day, clean up and be in bed by 6:00 AM. Randy was trapped. Again. Matters were made worse when his Networking company went out of business and he lost his bonus check. And things got still worse when the IRS came and seized the restaurant.

Randy was 30 years old. No house, no car, no job, no money in the bank, no credit cards, and he was $55,000 in debt, which seemed like millions to him at the time. He was borrowing money from friends, selling the furniture...

That's when Randy told himself, "You know, I'm never going to pay off this debt in the restaurant business. If I do, it'll take me till I'm 60. I've got to get back into Network Marketing."

Randy approached someone he had worked with in the past and asked him to lend him the $700 to get back in the business. Something he would never recommend anybody ever do, because it never works out. But Randy made it work out—for both of them.

Randy started to make his way back and he's never looked back. He's made millions in Network Marketing.

What got Randy's attention about this business from the very beginning was *leverage.* The former dishwasher knew all about trading time for dollars and the frustrated manager and failed restaurant owner knew there would never be enough time.

"I grew up poor and I hated it," Randy says. "I was running away from being poor as much as I was running towards being rich, but they both were motivating me. The idea of leverage, being able to bring some people in, teach them, train them, and get a residual override on their productivity was really sexy. I got that one right away."

But Randy didn't get the business right away. It took about five years of losing money, going to events, buying tools, and negative cashflow that caused him to really do some critical thinking. "Okay, I've done a bunch of different companies, had different sponsors, different product lines and different compensation plans, and none of them have worked. So obviously, this is either a total fabrication that they made up to get my money or it's on me."

The thing was that in all of those companies there were people who *were* successful. There were people who *were* making money and they had the same product line and the same compensation plan and the same everything that Randy did, and yet they went out and created success.

He realized, "it's not on the business, it's not on the company; *it's on me.*"

So, Randy made changes.

As said, he was pathologically shy, so he needed to work on that first. Randy read books and listened to audios that helped him be less fearful of people. He learned the skill of meeting people and placing himself in environments where he could do that in a non-threatening way.

Today, Randy realizes he's made millions of dollars just because he joined a softball league. He didn't join to make money. He loves baseball and just wanted to play ball. He wanted the exercise and thought it'd be a healthy thing to do. To his surprise, he discovered it was a safe and comfortable way to meet new people, too.

"It wasn't like being at a party where I would be standing next to the fern in the corner afraid that somebody would talk to me," Randy said. "You'd go there and get on a team and you'd meet 10 or 12 guys right away. And it wasn't about you or them, it was just about playing ball, so you got to know each other and become friends and let the relationship develop in a non-threatening way." He does the same thing now by taking college courses, going to the opera and with social media.

A real breakthrough for Randy was

getting clear that it doesn't matter if something works.

What matters is, does it duplicate?

When Randy understood that he had to do the business in a way that the people he brought in would be able to do as well—that was a watershed moment for him. He said, "Okay, I've got to do a step-by-step-by-step duplicable system that anybody—whether they're a PhD or a high school dropout like me, whether they're people who have experience or people who join in the business for the first time—can follow and build the business."

"Here's what you say when you talk to a prospect. Here's the first approach. Here's the marketing materials you give them. Here's the follow-up, and here are the marketing materials that go with that, and here's the follow-up after the follow-up, and here are the marketing materials that go with that."

Taking the time to conceptualize and put together this step-by-step system was a huge shift for Randy and it's made an extraordinary difference in the velocity and growth of his organizations and his income.

As with so many of The Greatest Networkers, Randy's #1 value is integrity. His people know he says what he's going to do and he does what he says.

When Randy brings someone in the business he makes a couple of promises. He tells them:

"I will never lie to you. And...

I will never knowingly tell you to do anything that's not in the best interest of your business."

The men and women on Randy's team know they can trust him. They know he's got their back. He thinks that's done more than anything to create the dynamic and loyal culture he's after in his international organization.

Another quality Randy emphasizes is having a good work ethic. He's willing to work. He understands it's not winning the lottery; there's no free money in this business. He knows that if he goes out and does the work, he'll build the income. Another word for it is self-discipline. Something Randy says is required in an all-volunteer business where most people are part-time and no one "has to" do anything.

Randy remembers reading the Stephen Covey book *Seven Habits...* 15 or so years ago. (He thinks he's read it 10 or 12 times.) One of the simplest things Covey urged was taking half an hour or 40 minutes on the weekend to get out your planner and lay out your week.

And when you're planning, Randy advises you dedicate most of your efforts for *rainmaker activities*. "We don't get paid to chat with people on the Internet and play Farmville," he says. "We don't get paid to clean off our desk and organize our briefcase or watch the recruiting video for the 87th time. We get paid when we meet people, make invitations, get them to presentations, and follow up." Rainmaker activities are simply actions that produce volume, because that's what Network Marketers are paid for.

What does Randy think it really takes to be a consistent million-dollar annual income earner in this business?

"Nobody's going to like the answer," he says. "It takes all you got. *All... You... Got!"*

"This is the hardest business you'll ever do," Randy says, "because you can't buy your way to success in Network Marketing. In other businesses you can have the right connections or you can con people and get by. In the corporate world, if you keep your head under the cubicle and just show up, you can make your way through."

"None of that stuff works in Network Marketing," he says. "This business is all about self-development. Your Network will only grow as fast as you do. I mean, I lost money for five years because I was a jerk. This is a business of accelerated personal development. If you want to be a multi-million-dollar producer, it takes all you got. "

"The good news is... all you got is enough."

The very best thing about Network Marketing for Randy is the thousands of people all over the world for whom he's been able to bring joy to their life, and they have been able to bring joy to his life.

"I've been able to mentor people who were living on welfare, raising their kids in the basement of a friend's house, who now make $30,000 a month. And it isn't the money really. The money's great, don't get me wrong, but I'm most excited for these people because it's the dignity it gives them, it's the freedom it gives them, it's the self-confidence it gives them, it's the belief it gives them."

"That's significance and that's what makes our business so amazing," Randy says.

"Network Marketing gives us an opportunity to create a legacy in very powerful and profound ways that you don't get to do in most other businesses. And that's really, really special."

The Transformation of Network Marketing

Sven Goebel was born in Hanau, at the river Main in central Germany near Frankfurt.

Sven's dad was an architect and a builder. His mother ran the office of their small construction and real estate company. Sven was their only child and describes his upbringing as "a nice, ordinary, conventional family environment." Growing up, Sven's mother was the force in his life. Never able to do the things she wanted to do herself, she was committed to making things different for Sven.

It wasn't about money, the latest clothes or "things."

Education was the key and Sven's parents invested heavily in his.

From the age of 11, Sven was sent abroad in exchange programs to learn languages and broaden his worldview. His parents came from a generation that wanted their son to have a great education, and one day to be hired by a great company and work there until retirement. But Sven's world was not the same as his parents and he decided early on his life would be different.

When Sven was a teenager of 18 or 19, he started thinking, "What are you doing after you finish school?" He knew he wanted a profession, one where he could deal with people, and he also wanted to do something with his hands. He'd spend his evenings and weekends in his garage, constructing things, fixing his bikes and mopeds, and he loved doing that. And, he wanted to make money. Lots of money.

So, Sven applied for a medical education at the university. Problem was, you needed the very best grades and Sven's were only second-best. He didn't get in.

What Sven did instead was to begin a science education in chemistry, planning to shift over to medicine later on. But he didn't have his heart in it. Sven's first six to 12 months at university were a dismal failure.

And that got his attention—at least his ego's attention. Sven told himself he either had to give it 100% or leave university.

He gave it the full 100—and he started to fall in love with his studies. Sven ended up with the best grades in his class and a Cum Laude Ph. D. But the effort was from his head. Not from his heart.

The big change in Sven's life came while he was working on his Ph.D. in 1992. A tennis partner and good friend of his had left university right after his exams, because of failing grades that would not allow him to do his Ph.D. As a chemical engineer he had started his own company. A year later this friend was a huge success, driving a BMW 850, living in wonderful villa apartments and spending more time on the tennis court than ever before.

Sven thought, "Wait a minute. Something's wrong here. Who has the great grades? Who failed? Who's really succeeded?" Sven wasn't jealous. Just wondering:

"Which side do I want to be on?"

It was at that same time Sven read a quote from Bill Gates, saying that all successful entrepreneurs employ college graduates—"The A students are working for the C students." Sven *was* on the wrong side. He suddenly had the deep desire for freedom and wanted nothing to do with being swallowed by a traditional job in the chemical industry.

Out of the blue, Sven got a call from a school friend inviting him to a Network Marketing presentation at a hotel in Frankfurt. It was just a small weekly opportunity meeting. It would change Sven Goebel's life for the better. For ever.

That night he learned there would be a huge event about two hours south of Frankfurt that coming weekend. The number one income earner in the company would be speaking. Sven and his friend decided to go.

There were hundreds of people in the room. It was a totally different scenario than they knew at university. Sven was sitting there in jeans with a leather tie, and a borrowed jacket surrounded by excited, ambitious men and women with sparkling eyes dressed sharply in business attire.

In the middle of the meeting, the back door opened on a scene Sven will never forget. A young man from Florida strode in. He had leather cowboy boots, a light green suit, carried a crocodile briefcase and was flashing a great big sparkling diamond wristwatch. He walked past in a cloud of cologne. Sven had never seen anything like him before. He was completely blown away.

The young man went up on stage and told the audience that he'd made seven million dollars in the business, starting off as a waiter working his way through college. He was 27 years old. His name was Jeff Roberti.

Sven turned to his friend and said, "Think about it. Can you and I together accomplish just 10% of what he's done? Are we capable of that?" His friend looked him straight in the eyes and said, "Definitely!" Sven said,

"That's $700,000. Let's get started."

They signed up that day.

Sven spent the first few months following the pattern his parents had set out for him: Investing in his education. The man who referred him to the business never actually joined, so Sven had no upline. He was totally on his own.

Ever the student, Sven read books. He found a cross-line group close to him and attended their meetings. Sven was a natural speaker and they put him on stage right away. Sven became a part of their organization without being in their pay line. That early experience gave Sven one of the cornerstones of his business philosophy.

"We all have to contribute. Not just to our own team. We are responsible for the overall success of the entire organization inside our company and, even more, to the total success of the whole of Network Marketing."

Sven struggled in the beginning because, he says, "I played it the hard way." He printed flyers, put ads into letter-boxes, knocked on doors, tried to get appointments in doctors' offices to place displays of the products. It was tough.

He did have some help. His dad really wanted this to work for him, so his father called all his friends and said, "When Sven comes and offers his product, purchase it, please. I really want him to succeed." Helpful, but that didn't really take Sven very far.

At a certain point Sven figured it out. He was able to ignite others when he talked about his vision. He found his passion and got really excited. Sven shifted his focus to the power of the business model and the possibilities it offered people for freedom and independence. He began to focus on people's "Why."

Sven began finding like-minded people who got carried away with the vision and his organization started to take off right away. Now in his second company, starting with just about the same team of people, the business grew explosively.

"Basically, what made us successful was focus and hard work." Sven says. "Doing the things we needed to do and sometimes, many times, didn't feel like doing."

Sven became a six-figure income earner in his 13th month. He was 29 years old.

Sven stayed with them for six years. Unfortunately—even though Sven's income had grown explosively and the company was a very, very well-known name—they went out of business. Today, being safe and secure in his business and being on top again, Sven is grateful for that experience. But at the time, the loss of such a significant income and having to start all over was pretty tough on him.

Sven attributes his success in the business to quickly building a solid infrastructure with weekly opportunity meetings, weekend trainings and a very simple system of daily actions he called KISS.

Sven took the old acronym for "Keep It Simple, Stupid!", and modified it into a daily action cycle of Kontakt ("contact" in German), Information, Start, and School. That was back in 1994 and Sven and his worldwide team still uses it to this day.

Sven's KISS system became super-charged when he shifted his focus from business-building to people-building.

Sven felt there must be more to growing a huge organization than prospecting, prospecting, prospecting. He was getting very interested in the subject of leadership, asking, "How do I get ordinary people—including myself—to become real, top charismatic leaders, one day running an organization that expands around the globe?"

What Sven figured out was...

"Business growth always follows personal growth."

Next question was: How to implement personal growth into the system?

Sven got the answer from the CEO of his company, Stewart Hughes, who gave a training called KASH, which stands for Knowledge, Attitude, Skills, and Habits. The combination of KISS and KASH intrigued Sven, and like a man with a Ph. D. in chemistry, he began to experiment. He developed, tested and refined the formula.

Today, that system is all mapped out. That's what he teaches. It's on his website, the tools are in place and organizations around the world—many outside of Sven's own company—are using it with their people and achieving great success.

The shift from a focus solely on building the business to becoming a "People Builder," led Sven Goebel to his mission today: Nothing short of "The Transformation of Network Marketing."

Sven's goal is to build a "bridge" for those outside the industry to come across into the profession by understanding the real values involved in Network Marketing. That integrity is what leads us. As we take away the hype, fluff and stories, and things start to become more authentic and real, Sven sees that "many, many more people will begin to follow those millions of invitations to join the profession that they've received from all those Networkers around the world."

That's what Sven loves to teach, and even more, to embody and to lead by example.

When Sven Goebel started out in Network Marketing two decades ago, he was 26 years old. He admits he wanted the money; the toys, travel, and the freedom and independence he was sure the business could bring him.

He was also a scientist and knew about physics. He saw the power of leverage right away and transferring that knowledge into making money was something that really appealed to him. He became "infected about the business model." Here was a way to become a business owner (as a student) without any significant cash in his pocket—and with so little risk.

Now that was something he could sell and excite a lot of other people about. And he's done that. Masterfully.

Today, Sven Goebel is comfortable with his company and he shares their goal to become a billion-dollar-plus player in the world market. He's always dreamed of being part of doing something great like that.

For himself, Sven wants to find out how many more people he can take to personal independence, total freedom and excellence before he's 60.

And he wants to take this industry much further than it is today.

Dr. Sven Goebel is committed to "The Transformation of Network Marketing," because as he sees it, that's the very best way to Transform the World.

Out of the Jar

John Haremza grew up in Perham, Minnesota, a town of 2,000 people a few hundred miles north of Minneapolis and about 70 miles south of Fargo, North Dakota. Cold country in winter. Very.

John's dad was the janitor at the high-school. His mom worked in the dog food factory. John was the youngest, and along with his brother and three sisters, the whole family lived with his grandmother until they'd saved enough money to have a home of their own. As John says, "We were poor, but I didn't know it."

John was a normal kid, "fairly aggressive" as he remembers, but happy—until he started school.

A popular book at the time was Dr. Rudolf Flesch's *Why Johnny Can't Read,* and that was this Johnny's problem. He couldn't. *Developmental reading disorder* is called dyslexia today. Back then they just called John "slow, dumb, stupid."

John remembers overhearing his dad telling a good friend how "stupid" his son was. He crawled into the doghouse, laid down with his beloved black lab and cried his heart out.

Each year of school just got worse for John. The teasing of grade school grew into taunting and tormenting. High school was humiliating. His teachers were frustrated and angry with him. Even John's parents thought he was slow and they worried about how he would survive in the real world when he could not even read a menu. "It was brutal," he says.

John Haremza didn't suffer from low self-esteem. He had *no* self-esteem!

John wouldn't say "hi" to somebody in the hall unless they said "hello" to him first. When John was forced to stand and read in class he read every word one at a time, *slowly.* His nickname was "The Robot." He became a total introvert. He tried to be invisible. (Life was less painful that way.) And he constantly tortured himself, asking, "What's wrong with me? What's wrong with me?"

Those were very difficult days.

Despite—or perhaps because of—his disability, John was a hard worker. He was good with his hands. That doghouse he'd crawled into he built all by himself. In his senior year of high school, John got on a work program with the city. At the end of his school day, he'd spend two hours mowing lawns; then he'd stay late and help the mechanics maintain the equipment.

The city manager who ran the street department was retiring and, based on his work ethic and how good he was mechanically, they offered John the job. He couldn't believe it.

$12,000 a year, right out of high school, John thought he had struck it rich!

But before John even began his new job, he got a call from the Barrel O' Fun Potato Chips people. They had an opening as a machine operator. One of the men at the city had told them about John. He went in for an interview and got the job.

John started working right away. He'd stay after work and help out in the maintenance department. Shortly, a position opened up in maintenance, so John became part of that department.

Nine bucks an hour. *Nine bucks!* John was in heaven. And so were his parents, because now John had a job and wasn't going to be dependent on them. (He was still living at home.)

A year into that job, John became the supervisor. He was very good at his job. Loved the work. Loved the people (and they loved him). He wore a beeper on his hip 24/7. Finally, John thought, "I'm important."

Nobody at the factory knew John was dyslexic. He hid it completely. He never told his workers what to do—and he never gave them written instruction. Instead, he would go work with them, hands-on, *showing* them what to do. He did that for four years. Then John learned about Network Marketing.

John's best friend Dan, home for the weekend from college, called and told John there were a couple of guys coming down from Minneapolis to talk about some water filters. He asked John to come listen to what they had to say.

John thought Dan wanted him to build a display or evaluate the quality or the price of the filters—certainly not to get involved in any type of sales. Not John, the dyslexic, self-esteem challenged introvert; the Invisible Man.

Due to a breakdown at the factory John arrived to the meeting two hours late in his blue shop uniform wearing a hairnet and smelling like potato chips. He saw the disappointment of "the two suits from Minneapolis" immediately. John knew what they were thinking, "We've been waiting two hours for *this* guy."

The "suits" demonstrated the water filter and the funky, yellow, nasty tasting water cleared right up, smell and everything. John thought it was magic. "Wow," he said. "This is unbelievable. Everybody needs one of these." John was so impressed he wrote a check on the spot for $480 and brought four filters home to show to his fiancée.

She, however, was not so impressed. It was the first week in December and they were getting married on the 17th.

John said, "Wait until you see what these things do." Problem was the water was perfect in his hometown. No change at all. His fiancé told him he'd been ripped off and he'd better stop payment on the check.

But John *had* seen it work and told her he wanted to buy 40 of these filters, which was going to cost another $5,000. Convinced John had lost his mind she threatened to cancel the wedding. John told her, "If I don't do this, and I run into somebody that did and they make a fortune... I don't know if I could forgive you for that."

John bought the 40 filters. He got his parents to cosign a note. Even before his filters arrived, John was out to a neighboring town in the dead of winter knocking on doors. He sold one his first week. It was the easiest $59 he'd ever made in his life. He just knew, "We were going to be rich."

John's older brother had also tasted the Kool Aid. He wanted to buy $5,000 worth, too. John told him, "I'll let you in on this deal, but we got to make a pact: We're not going to let anyone else know about this. I don't want to create our competition." John didn't understand the Network Marketing business model at all.

John's first breakthrough in the business came when a leader in his organization told him, "Listen, I made $200,000 last year—and if you told me I had to knock on doors to do it, I'd have never started." He showed John the concept of leverage. Instead of going out there and selling a filter for $179 and earning $59, John needed to offer people a money making opportunity for $5,000.

Shortly after that, John went to an event in Minneapolis where there were 1,000 people in the room. It was electric. A big guy with overalls walked across stage with one pant leg tucked in his boot wearing a baseball cap that was dented in the front. He told the audience he'd made $10,000 last month. That was all the money in the world to John. At that moment, John knew beyond any doubt...

"If that guy can do it, I can do it."

In his four-years with that company, John made more than $400,000. Today, in his 23 year Network Marketing career, John Haremza—a dyslexic, introverted, $9 an hour maintenance man with no self-esteem from just below Fargo—has earned more than $11.5 million dollars.

And John's message for everyone is: "If I can do it... You can do it."

So, what were the values and skills John had, or that he developed and practiced, that created such remarkable success?

John's clear that the core of his success in Network Marketing came from his belief. "People buy people," he says. "Your passion, posture, enthusiasm about what you're doing attracts and influences others." John thinks it was his sheer excitement that allowed him to sit down and talk to people, and even if they didn't really understand what he was doing they wanted to do it, too, because John was on fire.

The other thing John credits his early success to was his use of tools. "Your excitement grabs somebody's attention, then you let the tools do the persuading. John had an audiotape from his company. As John says, "If it moved I gave it a tape. If it didn't move I kicked it, then if it moved I gave it a tape."

He talked to anybody and everybody. John knew most people thought he was crazy. Didn't matter. He was looking for the person who thought, "What if he has something here?"

"I think one of the reasons I've had such success in this industry, " John said, "is I don't buy anybody else's story. I mean, look at my story."

> **"You need to have a desire to change your life. You can learn, everything else, but you can't put the heart in the lion."**

John's learned that if somebody doesn't have the desire, it's unlikely they're going to do what it takes to win.

As far as John's concerned, there was nothing magical about his success. "You've learned everything you need to know about Network Marketing in kindergarten. It's called show and tell."

"We tell stories about our company, about our products, about what's happened to us and what's happened to others." John learned the story by being involved; attending the meetings, listening to conference calls, and most importantly listening to audiotapes. John's car became his "university on wheels."

John understood the importance of relationships in this business from the very start. "Given my childhood," he says, "that was natural." He knew that people don't care how much you know until they know how much you care, and John genuinely cared about people and it came through.

John spent the next 12 years with that company and earned $4 million. Then he began all over again with a start-up company. It was "hand-to-mouth" in the beginning but in six and half years with his present company he's made more than $6 million.

"People are flea-trained," John says, relating a story he learned from Zig Ziglar. "If you take a jar and fill it with fleas and put the lid on it, the fleas go crazy—jumping, jumping, jumping—because they love to jump and they're trying to get out. But after hitting their heads on the lid time after time, they stop. They only jump high enough so they don't hit the lid. They've been conditioned. Take the lid off the jar and the fleas will never jump out. They'll die in there."

Network Marketing took John out of the jar.

John truly believes 90% of his success is the result of his working on himself; personal growth and development. Constantly trying to be better. Not settling.

Is that what it takes to be a million-dollar annual income earner?

"It's doing things right versus *almost* right. And doing it all—every day."

John speaks about setting the example. Caring about your people and belief. Put John in a company that he does not believe in and he's not going to be able to get other people to do it.

The best thing about Network Marketing for John is that he's got stardom *and* his life.

"Actors and athletes, the rich and famous, trade their freedoms for stardoms." John said. "In Network Marketing you can have that same excitement; you can be a star and still be just a real person, a regular guy."

What John Haremza loves most is that in Network Marketing you truly own your life. You're in control and you can live your life purpose. For John, that's classically short, sweet and real:

To have a positive impact on everyone he encounters.

Courage Comes From Caring

Donna Imson was born and raised in a small city high in the mountains outside of Manila, the capital of the Philippines. Her dad died when she was 12, so it was just Donna and her brothers growing up with their mom and grandparents. "It was an average life," Donna says. "There wasn't really anything worth noting about my childhood."

Donna married when she was 18. By the time she was 23 she already had three children. She dropped out of college to focus on raising them, but Donna's marriage didn't last.

"When you marry young, you don't really know what you're getting yourself into," Donna said. It turned out to be a difficult, dysfunctional marriage, but she couldn't leave, she wouldn't leave without the children. So for seven years she stayed in that abusive marriage.

"I was very much focused on my children," Donna says. "I felt like my purpose in life was to stay home and be a mom. I was happiest in that sense, but because of the nature of my relationship with my husband, it was impossible for me to have done anything else outside the home."

Donna made several attempts to leave, but she invariably returned. She was psychologically trapped in a vicious cycle.

The turning point came when Donna's husband turned on her daughter.

"I realized that it was not just me that was under threat, but it was also my children, and that spurred me into action," Donna said.

"By the grace of God and with the help of friends, I managed to leave for good. We had two bags and $10 to our name."

"We were moving from house to house for several months. I didn't want to be found. It was a very difficult time." And it was a defining moment.

Donna looked at her kids and knew she had to give them a better life.

There was nobody else they were going to be able to count on.

Despite the desperation Donna felt, she knew what she didn't want to do. If she got a minimum wage job—which with her lack of education and skills was all she could hope for—she would have to leave her children in the care of somebody else. She'd be paying most all of what she earned for someone to do what she really wanted to be doing. That just didn't make sense.

So instead Donna baked things and sold things and just tried to make do. She had moved back in with her mother, who lovingly stretched whatever resources she had to accommodate four extra people, so Donna didn't have to worry about rent or food. She had the temporary "luxury" of choosing not to have a job.

"My life prior to that moment was very average, Donna says. "I didn't excel in anything. I really didn't have any dreams growing up. I was a nobody. All I had was that one desperate need to make my children's lives better." That's what led Donna to Network Marketing, which she'd rejected back when she was still married.

"It's funny," Donna says, "because I really didn't get sponsored. I had a friend who would pick me and the kids up to go to a Vacation Bible School where we were both volunteering and he would tell me about this company he worked for."

"He sounded very proud of them," Donna says. "I asked him to tell me about it. It was Network Marketing. They happened to have a free registration period and that was the very last day. So, I didn't have to bring any money. I was desperate enough to try anything."

A couple of days after her friend called and said, "Okay, I connected you with so-and-so." Donna didn't know "so-and-so." She didn't have an upline, didn't know what to do to get started so... she didn't do anything.

But her mind had been opened. When another friend who really was active came and presented her with an opportunity, she readily said "yes." This time, Donna had an upline. First thing he told her to do was get to the meetings, and she did.

Donna went to meetings for three months. Every week. Finally her sponsor told her, "You know Donna, you're supposed to be inviting people to these meetings with you."

But she just couldn't invite anyone. Donna was terminally shy.

She didn't have any people skills and her abusive marriage left her emotionally challenged and socially handicapped.

Donna learned enough in those three months that when she finally talked to a friend interested enough to listen she readily drew circles on a piece of paper, and realized for herself, "I can do this." Her friend also realized that and signed up right then and there.

Donna started with that one friend. Every Saturday they would meet in her friend's house for a home meeting, and after a few months, the group started to grow. Donna became a bit more confident. She was able to do the same thing with another friend, and eventually another. The organization slowly grew bigger.

"Okay," Donna said, "let's keep doing this, and let's just keep doing it and doing it." It was neither fancy nor flashy.

She wasn't making a whole lot of money, but now she could afford the tuition and make sure her kids went to a proper school.

"Once I made the decision that I was going to do this business, and if I was going to do it, then I might as well do it right," Donna said, "the opportunities started opening up for me. I started seeing people. I started thinking of people. I started attracting people. Because I was in Network Marketing and I had my 'why' and that was very compelling for me—I got the courage to start talking to people."

There's a quote Donna loves by the Chinese sage, Lao Tzu, "From caring comes courage." That's really how Donna broke through and began to speak with people and grow her business.

Donna gave herself a manageable goal: To make sure she made one presentation a day.

"That was doable for me," She says. She could do that while the children were in school. "It didn't require a lot of time. I just made sure that I did that one presentation every day."

"Then on Saturdays, I'd arrange for somebody to watch the children for a few hours in the afternoon and I would have my group meetings. I just did that every week, week in, week out, the same thing over and over again." That's what Donna took responsibility for.

One of Donna's core values is responsibility. "The bottom-line was that I was where I was because of me. Not because of anything or anyone else—because of me and the choices I've made. So if I wanted to change, it was in my hands and nobody else's."

"In five years, Donna built a business that provided a monthly income equivalent to that of a bank manager's—a far cry from where she came from, but she was still living from paycheck to paycheck. Her confidence and skills were growing and so was the organization she was building with her mother.

Then out of the blue, the company's executives terminated her mother's distributorship. "I saw the dark side of the business, and it was like being hit in the solar plexus," Donna said. "My belief in Network Marketing was so badly shaken I stopped doing the business and considered quitting Network Marketing altogether."

Five months into Donna's "sabbatical," she attended a generic Network Marketing training event where she met Joseph Bismark, who went on to become her upline and founder of the company she's been with for 13 years now. "It was Joseph and our other founder, Dato' Vijay Eswaran, that saw what I was capable of way before I did," Donna said. "They worked patiently with me to help me become the leader that I am today."

Donna had an extraordinary opportunity to take a stand again for her value of responsibility when she was arrested and put in jail for the crime of... Network Marketing.

In the Americas and Europe, Network Marketing is a mature, accepted, even admired, business model. In many parts of the world, however, Network Marketing resembles the frontier days of the Wild, Wild West. In other parts, it's downright dangerous.

Donna was co-facilitating a leadership conference for her company. She respectfully declines to mention where this occurred, "because," she says, "it's a beautiful country and the people are just amazing." Donna was on her way to the airport when she was stopped by the police. They had been waiting, and asked her to go with them.

"I was in a strange land, didn't know anybody, didn't speak the language, thousands of miles away from anything familiar—and I was really afraid," Donna remembers. "But at the same time, I knew I'd done nothing unlawful." But she was wrong.

What should've been a matter that could have been cleared in a few minutes became an 11-month ordeal for Donna. She probably could have gotten out of jail sooner. There are things you can do with connections and resources. But Donna sensed that if the police didn't have her, they'd go after the other leaders in that country.

She decided to stay and fight it, to prove that her company and Network Marketing weren't scams. That in fact...

"Network Marketing is an opportunity that could be one of the greatest things that could happen for their country and their people."

"It was a necessary sacrifice," Donna says. "I know there were dangers, but at that point, I wasn't thinking of that. It was more important to make a stand for our company, for our people, for Network Marketing." Remember, "Courage comes from caring."

Donna feels that she found the belief she didn't have growing up and the gift of her life purpose through Network Marketing.

"Regardless of where you're from or who you are, you can do it," Donna says. "If a single mom, socially and emotionally handicapped, with no skills, no people skills whatsoever could make it, then anybody could—and that's especially important for women to believe, and that's become my driving force."

"The very best thing about Network Marketing is that it's for everybody. It's for people like me. It's for professionals, students. Whoever you are, regardless of your race, color, or creed, Network

Marketing is one of the most valuable opportunities to really transform lives."

"In Asia and Africa, where today it's all about reducing hunger and providing livelihood, you'll find scores of people wanting change, demanding change, but at the same time they don't really have much of an opportunity to make change happen."

"Well, here's Network Marketing."

"Who says that Network Marketing cannot make a difference in these countries?"

"There is a very big need right now for people to just *earn,* and I think that Network Marketing is the way for them to be able to do that. That's why I'm so very passionate about this business. It's just... I want to have more and more people realize they could really change their lives and the lives of the people around them through Network Marketing. And that they're worth it, just like I was."

"I am eternally grateful to God and to the people He's brought to my life, because otherwise, I wouldn't be who I am, where I am today.

"The courage I've had to make a change, to be the change, and stay with the change, came from their caring. And my desire is to inspire people to be the same, to the countless others out there in need of change."

Settle For More

Beth Jacobs was born in Groton, Connecticut, in the same year as her sister Ellen. They're only 11 months apart. She has two brothers, Harold and Craig. Allen, Beth's father was a career Naval officer; the Captain and Executive Officer of a couple of destroyers, and he served as Commander at Pearl Harbor, Chief of Staff of Naval forces in the Philippines, Chief Of Staff for Command Carrier in California and of Naval Forces in the Philippines, and Assistant Inspector General for the Navy in Washington, DC. The family moved a lot.

Beth went to elementary school in California, Georgia, Hawaii, junior high school in California and high school in Virginia and Rhode Island.

Her mom, Lennie, was a homemaker and also a Tupperware dealer for a couple of years when Beth was in 7th and 8th grade. "I think my dad wanted to quit the Navy and do Tupperware with her full-time," Beth said.

Knowing she would always find friends through joining the Navy's Officers Wive's Club or any social activity she did, Beth's mother mainly concentrated on their moves and making sure the four children found a friend the very first day they went to their new school. Beth can still hear her mother saying, "Invite them to dinner!"

The children all left the house on a mission, concentrating on finding some great new friends.

"We moved every year or two," Beth said. "I could move in a heartbeat, and adapt nicely, since I had those experiences growing up. And I learned basically that the same friends you're leaving are there in your next location, so I couldn't imagine not knowing new people and quickly making new friends at each place I moved."

"I was always happy," Beth said, "because I learned networking from my mother I was able to make friends easily."

Beth went to college at the University of Connecticut and got her Bachelor of Science and Master's Degree there. She did her Master's while teaching high school. She taught home economics, vocational education, business and she also taught history and psychology. There was a shortage of teachers the year Beth graduated, so she actually finished up college and taught full-time at the same time.

Beth taught for 10 years, and then started looking into doing something different. She learned about Network Marketing in business classes at college. From watching what the business did since she graduated, Beth was intrigued about the industry and she wrote the Direct Selling Association and got a list of 300 companies to look at.

Beth had been to an in-home cooking show when she was living in Illinois. That's the company she picked.

"I chose them 22 years ago," Beth said, "because it's something where I could showcase my love of cooking, baking and bringing families together to the table for mealtime. That was always important for the families where both my husband and I come from. Plus I had already seen that show and the products left such a good impression on me."

"While watching that first show, I remember thinking, 'Wow! I wonder if I could make money doing this.' But I didn't start my

Direct Selling business for three or four years after that. When I began it was really great, I think mainly because I set goals from the beginning."

"That's one thing many people don't do," Beth says. "And you can't have just any goal. You have to find a goal that is so powerful that every time you think of it, it's going to keep you inspired—inspired up. Since day one with my business my major focus was on cash for college for Jacqueline and Matthew, our two children, and retirement for Jake and myself."

"And everything I did with my business that was successful brought me that," Beth said, "even though they were long-term goals. I concentrated on the basics of the business. Our company only had 525 Consultants when I started, but luckily I attended a national conference in Chicago three weeks after I began, so I found successful Consultants there to speak with and learn from."

"I have a great work ethic," Beth says, "and when you work with conviction from day one, however you do it, things go great. Thank goodness for Bart Breighner's book *Face-To-Face Selling*. "What many people do is just read" Beth says, "but they don't apply what they read as something new to try for their business. I did that all the time, especially with that book. It was so important to me, every chapter."

"This business is all about face-to-face selling and prospecting."

"That really helped keep me focused on my goals," Beth says, "on what to do. And from teaching all those years I learned to be organized. And I'm pretty divergent and creative in my leadership. I do show people the way to get to success. And I learned there's more than one way to get there: Two plus two equals four, but so does five minus one, and four plus zero and six minus two."

"I just have everybody concentrate on the basics of the home party business. Offering the business opportunity to the host of the Show, then to the guests; finding the next bookings and selling the product; are the three areas of focus at the Show, before they walk out the door!"

"One of the first things I learned—and this was really an awakening for me, I didn't realize this would happen—was that not all people who signed up stayed with the business. Early on I learned I had to just keep recruiting new Consultants to my team, because my success will be determined by their life experiences and their success."

"I call it my success line," Beth said, "and I have about 6,000 in my success-line. My Personal Team and First through Third Generations make up my success line, however, I do train and support Consultants beyond that and earn about a half a million dollars a year."

"And I started out with my first commission check being $253.83," Beth said. "But at that time, I did not realize that there was a big opportunity until I began working the business and stuck with it. We are a home-party plan. That's how I got to where I am, by always doing my Shows."

Most people say you've got to work hard. Beth says it differently. She agrees that you do have to work, but you've got to work smart.

And working smart for Beth means following "The Best Practices" for your actual business.

She calls them RSVP, which are the best practices taught by her company.

The R is your personal Recruiting which she has always done. "I am always recruiting," Beth says. "Recruit one or two new Consultants per month minimum. At the Show is where I can bring people for training, and that's where I can build my team."

"But we didn't just start out by only me doing the recruiting. I wanted my team to recruit too, so I trained them to do that. So that's how you build your team wide and deep. I did that from the very beginning because I knew to do it."

S is Selling, always selling. Not just the minimums. Beth sells products and does her Shows, and she's made sure that those who she recruited and are on her team today are aiming to sell the leader's minimum of $3,000 per month.

V means working with the Very new people. "You never know who is going to be the next National Executive Director, which is my title and the highest title you can attain in our company," Beth said.

And the P means working with the Performers, the people who are matching their words with their actions and really doing something with the business. "RSVP should be your laser-focus!"

"You know," Beth says, "people want to do business with people. They want to do business with people who they know, like and trust. People I meet know I want to do business, and people want to do business with people who want to do business, so I figured that's something that goes along with the skill set."

"The other thing is, I think I'm really blessed to have had Jack Canfield's information when I was alone in the beginning," Beth said. "I mean, just the whole thing about 'Ask, Ask. Ask.' Because you're going to get what you ask for. And when you don't ask, the answer's always no. So it's always best to ask and find out what they are thinking!"

Ask Beth why she's so passionate about this business and she'll tell you that it's personal.

"It provides the opportunity to be a great mom and dad and earn an awesome income!"

"That's what I love most," she says, "and that it's a relationship business."

"One thing that I always tell people," Beth says, "Don't underestimate the business. There really isn't a need that has to be created for our industry. That need already exists."

"We have increased our Direct Selling businesses every year for 22 years," she says. "So, I think the best tips I can give people are when you're trying your Network Marketing business or any home-party plan or Direct Selling, always give yourself permission to succeed.

"Settle for more."

"I mean," Beth says. "It doesn't matter where you are in life. Just give yourself permission to move forward; don't look back; you're not going that way. Don't let anything hold you back. Just decide, whatever your past, don't make excuses, because you can't make excuses and money at the same time."

"Find a goal. It has to be a very powerful goal that sets you on fire and keeps you inspired. The goal keeps you there and it makes you work smart. Sometimes you have to move on to plan B, plan C… Just be laser-focused!"

"The number one reason I found for why someone doesn't get involved in this industry is because someone didn't ask them."

Make it your goal to ask everyone and let them make a decision for themselves."

"When you don't ask, whose choice it?" Beth says. "It's your choice and it should be theirs. It's so easy to match our business with the needs of a person when you first talk with them and find out what they're looking for."

"This industry is a definite opportunity and when the opportunity arises, just go for it. Be the best you can be by confronting the opportunities you have each day. You have the opportunity to control your own money and time! I don't know any other business that you could start up for such a low cost. And I just don't want anybody to underestimate this great opportunity just because it does cost so little to start this business."

"You can control your life and will get everything you want and you'll have the opportunity to be a mom or a dad and earn the money that you desire, dream of and deserve simply by helping enough others get what they want!"

"With Network Marketing, you *can* be happy with your job. We earn what we want to earn."

"I'm really passionate about this industry. It's the career of the 21st century."

"The only reason why I'm here today is because I've helped others get what they want, and it made an ordinary person like me lead an extraordinary life. Network Marketing is an absolutely amazing career choice!"

How You Do Anything Is How You Do Everything

Donna Johnson grew up in Appleton, Wisconsin. Her dad ran a printing press and a paper mill. He left the family when Donna was 13, moved to California, opened up print shops there and became a millionaire. He never sent any money back to Donna's mother.

"My father was a misogynist (a man who hates women)," Donna said. "He thought my brothers were awesome, but believed my mother and I were not good people and he treated us both badly."

Donna learned a lot about how not to act or behave as a parent from that. She watched her mother have a nervous breakdown, because she had no skills to support the family. They were forced to go on welfare. Donna and her brothers started working as preteens to bring in money. Donna remembers thinking to herself...

> **"I never, ever want to be in a position where I'm so helpless."**

Growing up, Donna could've gone either way: She could've been a really bad girl and proven her father right, or she could have become an overachiever to prove him wrong. Donna chose the achiever.

She poured herself into her goals as a competitive swimmer. She would be up at five going to the Y to work out. "In the middle of January, it's pretty darn cold in Appleton, Wisconsin," she remembers. By the time she was 18 she competed and was ranked on a national level for two years. Donna didn't go on to college. She became a swimming coach instead.

She was only 19 when one of her friends invited her to a makeup party. Donna watched the woman demonstrating the cosmetics and she thought, "Wow, what a great way to supplement my income. I could be coaching and doing this to make some money. Maybe buy some clothes. Maybe travel."

It just looked like a fun way to earn extra income to Donna: Go out, have these parties and meet people. All she knew then was that there was a commission you could earn from selling the products. The more she got into the business, the more she realized that you could generate significant residual income by building a team, and she became even more excited.

Donna was married at 20 and she began her family right away. First was Nathaniel (now 31 years old), then Nicole (now 29), and Joe (27), and later she would add the twins Alex and Livi (now 17) —five more reasons she had a passion to succeed in her business.

Donna was really eager to achieve the top position in the company and earn a car. One night, a corporate leader was doing a training session on goal-setting and she wanted everybody to share their goals for the year. She knew about Donna's goal and handed her the microphone first. Donna was seven months pregnant (with Joe). She stood up and said, "I'm so excited. I am going to qualify for District Director."

Donna was just oozing enthusiasm about achieving that position and all that was happening in her life and business. But as the microphone went around the room, one by one the other women said, "Well, my family is number one. They're what's most important. I'm not going for that position. I'm happy where I am, because my children come first."

The gist of it was that Donna was not a good mom, because she wasn't putting her family first.

Donna felt like someone stuck a knife in her. "What?" She thought. "I'm doing this business *because* my family is the most important thing. My family is number one to me."

"No, I'm not going to listen to any that," she told herself. "I'm going forward *for* my children. I'm going to press on and reach this position—and more, much more!"

Donna never looked back. She remembers that as a defining moment. She could've easily succumbed to the peer pressure. But she made the choice to take action, knowing in her heart and her gut that she was doing the right thing.

Ever the achiever, Donna did very well in that company. By her early 20's, she already reached the very top position. Then, she became a student of the profession. She started learning about all the Network Marketing opportunities that were out there.

She was 29 years old when, based on her research, she changed companies. Donna has now been with her company for 20 years. She is their #1 income earner averaging $2 million a year.

"What I always did right was connecting with people," Donna says. "I love building relationships and knowing that something positive might come of it. Something might not, but that's my job, to make friends regardless of the outcome."

Donna emphasizes the importance of being authentic—connecting with people in a way that they know you, like you and trust you. Letting them know you're not perfect and you're comfortable sharing your struggles as well as your successes. "You know," she says. "I've been there. I know how you feel. I felt that way too, and here's what I found helped me." Donna wants people to feel...

"Hey, you did it, I can do it too."

One of Donna's keys to success is that she's been very, very diligent about her calendar and daily activities—something that has not changed over the 30 years that she's been in the profession.

"I always share with people, 'If you handed someone your calendar, would there be evidence that you're committed and that you're actually in this business? Or are you working your business in your head? Are you doing it as a hobby when you really want to be making an income? Hobbies cost money. Businesses make money.'"

Donna believes you have to do your due diligence so that you truly understand the opportunity that you have, because, "That's when this business is going to really get in your blood and in your heart."

"When you really believe in what you're doing," she says, "you're going to actually do the activity. And when somebody tries to, you know, steal your dream or make fun of you or whatever, you're going to be able to overcome that. You've got to do the due." And...

> **"You have got to get in front of people and tell them the story about your business."**

"I believe in leading with the opportunity along with your product," Donna says. "Of course, your product is a big piece of that opportunity, because you get to market a great product as *part* of the opportunity. You've got to get in front of people. Lots of people. This truly is a numbers game. If you want to go quickly up the ranks in your company, you've got to get in front of more people to tell the story."

"And not everybody is going to be interested," Donna admits, "but you're going to make friends, you're going to find out if they know someone that is looking to diversify their income, and you're going to be able to offer them something else if they're not interested in the business. Maybe they want to be a preferred customer. Maybe they want to use the product. Maybe they want to host a get-together for you and help expose other people to what you're doing. "

The most important thing Donna wants everyone to know—whether you are entry level consultant/distributor in the early ranks of your business, or you've made it to the top—is that you need to get out there and make friends, schedule appointments and tell the story— whether in a group, one-on-one, or a combination of both— or networking, or through social media.

"A lot of people start this business alongside their primary job." she says. "You can do that. You're going to be real busy, but you're also changing your life and you're going to give yourself options so that you can raise your income to the level of your job."

And then Donna says you make choices: "Maybe you want to walk away from that job. Maybe you want to lower your hours. No matter what choice you make," she advises, "you have to be committed to your goals and see them through. You are going to have rejection. You are going to have doubts. You have to discipline yourself to work through them."

Donna says most people definitely overestimate what they can accomplish in their first year and underestimate what they can make in five years. She personally knows a number of people that, if they would have simply stayed involved would be millionaires today. The only way you can fail in this business, she says, is quit.

Donna Johnson has made a fortune in Network Marketing. She never has to work another day in her life.

So, why is she still doing it?

"It's great to get there," she says, "but when you lead people there with you, the satisfaction of that, knowing that you've made such a difference. Wow!"

"I mean, it's like watching your kids graduate," she said. "You know, when you graduated it was like, okay, ho hum. But when your kids graduate, you're in the audience sobbing, right? That's how it is with this business."

One of Donna's neighbors, Dianne, decided to do the business. Her husband Dave was not real thrilled. He said, "She just wants you to be successful, because she'll make more money." He did not like Donna or Network Marketing at all.

Dave got promoted and moved the family to Portland, Oregon. He eventually softened and told Dianne, "Okay, honey, if you're going to do this, then *really do it.* Tuesday and Thursday night, go out, do your business, I'll be home with the boys."

Today Dianne is at the very top of the company and doing very, very well. One day last year, Dave called Donna and he literally had her in tears.

He said, "You know, I can't begin to thank you for the difference you've made in our family. My bride is so amazing. To see the growth that she's had, and the financial contribution she's made, and the pressure that has taken off of me. We won the trip, too." (It was to Italy and Greece.) It… I'm… We're going, and it's my 50th birthday, and I have a sister that lives in Rome and a sister that lives in Switzerland."

"Because of you, we're going to be able to celebrate my birthday together. They're flying down; we're going to see each other for the first time in years."

"Thank you Donna. Thank you for sharing this. And thank you for never giving up on my wife and believing in her even when I didn't believe in this, and I was trying to protect her from you and I thought you were the 'evil woman.' I'm so, so grateful, I can never thank you enough."

"Those are the kind of phone calls that rock my world," Donna says.

Donna loves the person she's become and continues becoming. She's a student, learning and getting better every day. "One of the greatest gifts you can give your children is the gift of having *them watch you* build a business from home," Donna says, "manage your expectations and disappointments, setting goals, and connecting with people."

"I love the lifestyle of being able to live my day and week and month the way I choose," she says. "I choose my travel schedule. I don't do alarm clocks very well, so I get up when I'm done sleeping. I just love the choices I have and the freedom."

"And what I love most," she says, "is when I'm mentoring someone, an up-and-coming leader, I tell them that I'm mentoring them to become one of *my* mentors. Every single person on your team brings something different to the party, like the different parts of the body have different functions. I mentor people to be my mentors and I think that's why I've got such an amazing team."

"I mean, they're rock stars. I'm blown away. It just brings tears to my eyes when I look at our convention arena and most of the people are from my team. It's humbling, and then you see the leaders that speak on stage and... I'm like a proud mama."

Changing People's Lives

Frank Keefer didn't come from an affluent background. In fact, he didn't experience indoor plumbing or electricity until he was about six years old when he moved to the city. Frank was a "war orphan" from World War II. He grew up on a tenant farm in western Maryland, then went through the public school system in Baltimore and was self-supporting by the time he was 15 years old.

Frank expected he had no options for the future outside of flipping burgers or driving a delivery truck, so his goal was to go in the military. He figured he would spend a career there. That would give him an opportunity to see the world and "be somebody." Frank enlisted in the Marine Corps and a couple of years later, the Vietnam War broke out.

He went to Vietnam. "As an infantryman," he said, "you had about 100% chance of being killed or wounded." Frank says he "enjoyed the latter" several times.

He decided the military was not the career for him.

He went to college. Paid for 100% of it himself, because "the GI Bill was insignificant in those days."

"I was one of the first returning Vets to go to school," Frank said. "In those days, the teachers had to sign-off on the fact that you were actually attending class. It was just a brutal environment for a veteran. So, I dropped my veteran status and I went through as a war orphan, which actually paid me 10 dollars more a month. That was a lot of money in those days."

"And the interesting thing was, I barely made it through high school," Frank said. "I think part of that was because I worked 50-60 hours a week, but in college because the environment was so harsh, I was determined to get through as quickly as I could. I drove a cab at night in Baltimore city. Got through in two years and graduated with honors."

By that time Frank was married, had a child and he thought his leadership experience in the military, his scholastic record, and the fact that he was married would help him secure a job. But in those days, people just weren't interested in hiring veterans.

So Frank got a job building furniture for Montgomery Ward. His take home pay was $48 a week, $3,000 a year. Finally, Frank got a "real" job teaching 12th grade. He really enjoyed that. He taught political science.

At that time, his brother was missing in action in Vietnam, so Frank went back in the military with the intention of finding him. This time he went into the Army and got involved in the Special Forces and went through the Ranger School. He received a direct commission for Combat Leadership, but by that time the war was winding down and Frank could see that promotional opportunities were going to be limited.

So, Frank left the military again and went back to teaching. But he was transferred to the 7th grade, which for him was like baby-sitting. He bailed out of that and started climbing the corporate ladder.

Over the next 15 years, Frank worked for seven Fortune 500 corporations, seven multi-billion dollar companies and a bunch of start-ups.

"I would do extremely well," he says, "making over half a million dollars a year, but I'd reach the point where my reward was either increased sales quota, decreased commissions or diminished territory. I woke up in Kansas one day and had no clue where I was. I decided, 'That's it. I'm done.'"

Frank walked away from corporate America with no job prospects. He decided he was going to go into business for himself. He wanted to work at home, which was a very unusual concept at the time for somebody with Frank's corporate background.

"I met my wife when we were both 40 years old," Frank said, "and when I got married, I told her, 'If you let me work for a couple years, I'll make enough money and we'll retire.' I worked several years on a contract that was to pay us about $8 million and bought an expensive piece of property. The multi-billion dollar company decided to renege on paying. All they gave me was a $50,000 buyout. We had to liquidate our life's savings to pay the debt on the property. So when I walked away from corporate America, I didn't have a dime and I had no prospects.

"I came home and told my wife I'd quit and she said, 'That's okay.' I said, 'You don't understand. We don't have any money. We'll probably end up living in a tent.' And she said, 'I'd prefer a tree house.' Those were her exact words. And I said, 'You really don't get it,' and she said, 'You'll think of something.' The confidence that I had from my wife was unbelievable."

It was around that time Frank was introduced to Network Marketing.

"I immediately saw the leverage and the opportunity of a production-based commission system."

So he got involved. That company had one of the more difficult pay plans, but Frank saw if you hit the top level, you were worth millions and millions of dollars a year. "I never achieved a level that I wanted to with that first company," Frank said, "but I was on my way."

"The important thing to remember is that it was an apprenticeship," Frank says. "A lot of people get into a Network Marketing business and they don't enjoy success overnight, and they don't understand that anything you do—I don't care if it's a carpenter or a heart surgeon—there's an apprenticeship program that you have to go through until you learn what you need to."

"I look at everything that I've done," Frank says, "whether it's in martial arts or sky diving or anything else where I've achieved top levels, and it took years and years of studying and practice. Network Marketing is no different."

Frank went to work with a couple of Networking companies, gong to the top of each one. He was terminated by one company. He didn't do his proper due diligence on another, learning later the owner was "a crook, " so he bailed out. At that point, he was done with Network Marketing, but Frank inadvertently stumbled onto his current company.

"At first I thought it was same old, same old," he says, "but they did have a unique compensation plan that was designed for the statistically average person. I could see that you could almost be an idiot and be successful."

"Once I saw that the pay plan really worked, I decided to go for it," Frank said. "I used the organizational management skills that I had developed in the military and in corporate America, and I very selectively recruited people. It wasn't too long before I had people coming out of the woodwork to join up with me, but I probably turned down 90% of them."

"I wouldn't bring anybody in that I didn't think couldn't hit $100,000 a year annualized within their first 12 months."

"And so I went on in and that's what happened. I was very successful. Of the first 10 people that were in my group, eight of them had over a quarter of a million annualized within their first year."

Frank's income went up dramatically. He was almost at a million dollars a year. "In my 37th month," Frank said, "my heart pooped out on me and I was told I wouldn't make it out of the hospital, but I did. And I'd reached a level where I'd never have to work again."

That was 15 years ago and Frank's company has continued to pay him since then, and he's worked to the degree that he can.

"I enjoy the business," Frank says. "It's a people-oriented business. It's no different than corporate America. You're really a problem solver. People identify their problem or you help them identify their problem, then it's your job to provide a solution for it—whether that solution is time or money or a product. It's all just conversational marketing."

"The reason I got into this business in the first place was I wanted to be with my wife, Gingie, pure and simple," Frank said.

"I was a kid that grew up with nothing and I'd reached the point where I had the Mercedes, the gold Rolex Presidential, all that stuff, and it just dawned on me one day that it didn't mean anything. I was in my late 40s. I just thought, 'What the heck am I doing? Who cares about all this money? It's not worth it.' I wanted to spend time with my wife and savor my life."

"And that desire hasn't changed," Frank said. "But I'll tell you, for a couple years, when I couldn't work at all, I really I missed it. It was like, 'What have I done lately? Whose life have I changed lately?'"

"Because that's what this is really all about: Changing people's lives."

"When you take somebody that has the desire, but hasn't made it… I got a fellow out in the Great Northwest, he'd been married for 18 years, working 80 hours a week, and he never saw his family. And today he's a million-dollar earner. He's with his family all the time now."

"I had a gal the other day," Frank said. "She came in this business when she was 18 years old. She actually lived in a tent in the woods with her mother, and I believe she had five or six siblings. There was no father around."

"The mother came into my business and then the daughter. She didn't have a lot of, you know, social influence or anything, but she stayed with it. She's now a million-dollar earner. There's a lot of self-satisfaction in that for me, because that's two generations of people's lives that I may have had some positive influence on."

"When they come up to you with tears in their eyes, and thank you for the fact that they're together as a family, you can't put a price tag on that," Frank said. "And of course they're the ones that did it. I didn't do it. But they look to me and to others I'm sure, as more than a causal factor, but as the one that actually did it for them, which again isn't true. You know, everybody that's successful does it on their own. But there's just nothing like that."

"You know, I've run into people in airports that I don't even know, that have thanked me for changing their life and it really gives you a sense of purpose. It becomes addictive. You almost crave that. I do."

Frank Keefer's life purpose is to help as many people as he possibly can, realize there's more to life than they currently are aware of.

"And I arduously approach that," he says. "I mean, I think about that every single day."

The question Frank always asks people is, "What do you really want to do with your life? You're really only here one time. What do you want to do with it? Are you going to make a difference?" And he's very serious about that.

"I realized early on that everything I had done in my life had led me to the point where I've found a business that truly was who I am."

Frank Keefer has helped more than 300 people become million-dollar earners in his company.

"Somehow they saw some inspiration," Frank says. "Something that I did made a difference in their lives, and you can't really put a price tag on that type of psychic income."

"I'm working now, not for the money, because I'm fortunate enough to be comfortable, but it's just a great feeling when you change somebody's life.

"That's why Network Marketing is such a great business. That's why I absolutely love it."

I Can Powerfully Affect People

Robert Middleton grew up in Charlottesville, Virginia, "with a silver spoon in my mouth and one in each hand," he says. But at the time he was growing up, Bob didn't realize that.

He lived on a 744-acre Hereford cattle farm thinking "everyone knew what dirt smelled like." It was his grandparents' estate. They were industrialists and they founded a company called Babcock and Wilcox (B&W) back in 1856. The property is currently the site of the University of Virginia's Birdwood golf course.

It was a *big* farm. They had stables, a dairy and cows, sheep, horses, even Hereford show cattle. They did 55,000 bales of hay every season. Bob grew up loving the machinery and the tool houses, and sitting around the potbellied stove with all the farm hands from all over the world. Real true cowboys teaching him cowboy talk, which was mostly four-letter words. As a little boy, Bob had a ball.

"I just didn't know we were wealthy," he said, "and my mom made sure that we had a normal life and normal friends and weren't ostentatious—and that we were nice folks. She was a lovely, down-home lady from West Virginia. She had no airs. Everyone loved her."

When Bob was 14 his parents got divorced. His mom kept her four boys and that was about all she got. They went from riches to rags.

Bob ended up being raised mostly by his godfather who taught him one thing above all—how to work, *hard.*

Bob went to college in Virginia and got drafted during Vietnam. Everybody he knew that was in the draft lottery had put two quarters in a jar and Bob drew the lowest draft number, so he won the pot—$48.25 in quarters. The only thing he'd ever won in his life. He was so excited he forgot he was being drafted.

Bob, who had never been on a jet plane, flew to Chicago and then to boot camp in Kenosha, Wisconsin. It was February. It was 25 below zero some days. It was not fun. And somehow he ended up in Seattle, Washington, at a deep-sea diving school.

When he got out of the military, Bob went back to college in Virginia, finished that and promptly moved to the Cayman Islands. He bought some property there and had a hull inspection service for an oil transfer company.

"No one told me it took real money to live down there," Bob said. When he ran out of money, he moved up to Atlanta and started in the construction industry. Pretty soon he had a couple crews working and was framing houses during the big housing boom.

Bob worked for Rutenberg Homes out of Florida "I built the houses, they collected the money," he says. He did that for five years and learned about business, specifically about budgeting and planning.

"I learned about making a list every night for what you're going to do the next day," Bob said, "and picking the top six things that are income generating *and* grabbing the one you absolutely don't want to do and doing that first. To this day I make lists every night."

Bob still plans his work and he's still focused on income generating activities.

And the budgeting he learned taught him how to manage his affairs and never forget from whence he came. Even when Bob was making big money in Network Marketing (and a couple of million a year for many years is big money) he didn't go crazy. He saw the people around him. The money just made them more of what they already were.

"Being in the construction industry and dealing with the public as clients, building a house for people, it's quite a relationship," Bob says. "It's very similar to Network Marketing; building an organization and having those key player relationships."

How did Bob get involved in Network Marketing? He reluctantly went to an opportunity meeting.

"A friend of mine, Steve, called me and kept bugging me to go to this meeting," Bob said. "I had moved into building material sales and he was one of my biggest clients. So I said, 'If you'll buy me lunch, I'll listen to anything you say.' I hated eating alone."

"So, he bought me lunch and kind of started drawing circles, and... I was bored to death. Then he said, 'Look, we need to go to a meeting.' And I said, 'If you will never mention Network Marketing to me again, I will go to any meeting you want.' And I went."

There were a couple of hundred people in the room. They played a video with some country music by Rex Allen on it and the guy in the front of the room had white hair that was swept way back. He had been a funeral plot salesman. Bob was "kind of" impressed, but not *really,* and he wasn't *really* paying attention either.

And then, at the very end of the meeting, they gave Bob's friend Steve an award for earning $16,000 in one month.

Bob had never made $16,000 in his life in one month—in anything. That finally got his attention.

He signed up immediately.

"The reason I came into the industry," Bob said, "was because I actually saw his check and I knew he was lazier than me. I knew I didn't make that much working 70-80 hours a week. I looked at it as a big step up and a way to make more money with less effort."

"When I started doing the business, I really loved dealing with the people," Bob said, "They weren't all building houses, they had much more varied interests than just windows and doors. It was a real relationship with them, instead of order taking, which was what I had in the building material industry."

Bob out-earned Steve and went on to be one of the top 20 producers in that company. He quickly realized the freedom the money brought, being able to pick whom you work with and when you work—and the travel. He says it was, "just a complete lifestyle upgrade."

Still, Bob was searching for the secret to success in the business. He asked one of his mentors, industry legend Jeff Roberti (who's gone on to earn over $70 million in his Network Marketing career). "What's the big secret about making huge money?" Jeff said, "There is no big secret. You model the ones that are doing it. Wrap your personality around that after you learn the basic skill sets and the business systems. Then teach others to do the same—and *don't change anything.*"

So that's what Bob did.

Once he found someone who said, "I really want to build this, I've got 20 or more hours a week and I'm teachable. What do you want me to do?" Bob would put them into his strategic organizational development plan.

He would start by telling them, "Go out and bring people into your business: Recruit people for 30 days, full bore, full-blown, flat-out personal recruiting."

"Success is in the show."

"Your success is based upon how many people you show your product and your business to," Bob says. "Not how many people you help building their group. It's based on your personal income generating activities."

"At the end of the first month, after you take all-out massive action, you pick your top producer. The best attitude, the most teachable, which," Bob says, "is the number one key in the industry. You find the one that's doing the most business."

"There are two kinds of people," Bob says, "those that make excuses and those that make money. The ones that are producing, and are the most teachable I invite into a mentor relationship for the second month. So, the first month they were recruiting and they've proven they know how."

"The second month I'm going to have them repeat their activity. They're going to take 80% of their time and they're going to recruit just like they did the first month. But the 20% of their time that they're not recruiting, I'm going to teach them to teach their number one person from last month how to recruit."

"That person is going to duplicate momentum through the leverage of system-based leadership. Next month I'm going to teach them to teach their strongest; and the leader ranks begin to increase and group momentum begins. Then the person they were in mentorship with last month, who they taught to go out and teach to recruit; now I'm going to teach them to teach to recruit. I'm going to teach them about advanced event promotion, about developing cities, about developing geographic areas, maybe even international. I'm going to teach them about newsletters..."

"There are three different skill sets," Bob says. "Getting started in building personal momentum, duplicating that momentum by taking a person that you've started in your business who's proven themselves, that's teachable, and teaching them to duplicate that skill set. Then you take the strongest person and teach them to duplicate that, to build a self-sustaining, self-motivating cash-flow organization."

"It takes three generations of leaders to duplicate that," Bob says. "And once they go through one cycle, that organization will make you money for the rest of your career in that company. Three months to build an organization that's a stand-alone income generator. I would build however many organizations I needed based upon how much money each group's momentum produced."

"And that's what I did and it worked perfect."

According to Bob, what it takes to become super-successful in Network Marketing is consistency of income generating activities wrapped around a very simplistic strategy that works and that can be duplicated.

"You can't control people's behavior," he says, "but you can, through the sifting and sorting which happens when everyone enters a duplicative business process, find the ones who have the level of desire and are teachable enough to follow the system."

"Staying consistent and doing the job every day is really, really important. Two million dollars a year is earning $166,000 per month, which is $16,600 override on 10 key duplicating distributors. Finding the compensation plan to pay this type of override is the key," Bob said. "The ideal plan should pay a predictable amount of money on each order to unlimited levels with minimal qualifications. Distributor-friendly plans are a relatively new concept, but they are evolving."

"It's not hard to make $1 million."

"First you have to earn $10,000 utilizing a system that can be duplicated: Establishing personal momentum. Then you expose that system to everyone and teach the producers who show up and start duplicating that system: Group momentum. Understand that the best picker wins. Then you teach them to teach and develop group momentum and your income will exponentially follow. Then you do it again."

"I figure no one's getting out of here alive," Bob says. "And when I get out of here I'm going to have the legacy of whomever I affected through my deeds and actions. I'm going to have the people who I know I helped. Network Marketing allows me to do that. I can go out and earn income and I can powerfully affect people."

"Network Marketing is a contributory business model."

"To be able to watch people change and to know, privately and personally—and humbly, that your time and interaction may have had a directive hand in that, it's a reminder of the real rewards beyond the money; that you can contribute to people's lives."

"That's what this business is all about," Bob says. "The rest of it is just stuff. When you can affect people, and they you, and experience fellowship and good times during the building process, that's when the real fun starts.

That's why I do all this. That's what it's all for."

Exciting Adventure

Warren Nelson grew up in Kansas City, Missouri. He was the oldest of five children born to "very young, struggling, selfless, enduringly good parents who were pretty far below the poverty line," he says.

The year Warren was born, his dad started undergraduate school. He painted in the daytime, running a crew, and went to night school to get a law degree. His mom worked as a registered nurse from 11:00 PM to 7:00 AM—put the kids to bed, worked all night, got up and got the kids back up. Warren says he has no idea when she slept.

"They took on too much," Warren says. "They were overwhelmed."

"My mom left my dad behind in Kansas City and went back to Wisconsin with the kids when I was in sixth grade. By then she'd had a fifth baby. My dad followed after and was depressed for 10 years because he had given up his dream of a law practice."

"So there was this combination of his dream being crushed," Warren said, "their hard work, their goodness and their selflessness. They were broke. What little they had they devoted entirely to the children."

"Fortunately kids have their own resources," Warren said. "You know, in their community, at school, if they at least have enough to eat and have some clothes. So we kids all pursued the strategy of high achievers: Academically, class leadership, sports, all that. It was then, as a kid, I actually found my passion."

"I was a 12-year-old guy in a small town," Warren said, "delivering newspapers on his bicycle. And old Herb, the sales manager, called me in and said, 'Hey Warren, about 10 years ago there was a paper boy here in town... The *Milwaukee Journal* is going to have a contest. You can write up new subscriptions to the paper.' Then he added, "And that guy 10 years ago? He won a whole roomful of prizes."

"Herb painted a picture for me," Warren said, "I played Little League and I had this old dumb glove that didn't even have rawhide for the fingers. Herb said, 'You can win a glove and a bat, baseballs, fishing rod and reel, fishing tackle, tennis racket.' Then he said again, 'This fellow, 10 years ago, had a whole roomful of prizes.' I was absolutely entranced by that vision."

"So he sent me out and I sold subscriptions on my paper route, and then after all the other boys said they'd sold all they could, Herb told me, "Okay, you did the best on your route, so now you can go all over the whole city, no matter who's route you go to,' And he told all the other boys and they were all fine with that, because they knew nobody could sell any more subscriptions in that town."

"He picked me up in his car and we'd go out and he said, 'Okay, go down this street. There's somebody that doesn't subscribe. Go talk to them.' I kept signing up subscriptions at kind of a record pace."

> **"He never gave me a single bit of training—no script, no approach, nothing. All he did was paint that picture and I did better and better and better."**

"Long story short," Warren said, "I won the contest for the whole state of Wisconsin. They flew me in to watch a professional baseball game in Milwaukee. I had my picture taken with the governor. All I did, you know, I just worked hard at this thing, because I wanted to be in a roomful of presents. And it was an adventure. Exciting. I loved it."

"What I learned was I had some passion for that kind sales and achievement," Warren said, "but I never pursued that because I thought technology would be my way out. That's what my mom told me. You know, the space race was on and they said you could make a lot of money in science and engineering. That's how I was going to avoid the kind of grinding lifestyle my parents got trapped into."

"So, I went into the wrong field," Warren said. "Got a Master's Degree. I just drove myself, night school, working full-time in the design and development of jet engines, and I married my college sweetheart, too."

"I learned a lot about what it extracts from you to subjugate your real passion," Warren said. "I know the spiritual and emotional penalties. At that point I decided that project management, development, science, mathematics wasn't for me anymore."

"So I went back and got an MBA at Harvard Business School, went into marketing and sales. There you have unlimited upside, you produce, you travel, more adventure. And that takes me right up to when I got involved in Network Marketing in 1988."

"My wife Mary plays a big part in my life and career," Warren said. "She was a big hitter with Re/Max in the Chicago suburbs. She worked way too hard. She came home one night and said she'd found something to do where she could get out of real estate."

"Honestly, I only looked into Network Marketing to keep Mary from doing it."

"So that Saturday I had my first ever exposure to the business. I went to this meeting and John Sexsmith was the presenter. He was a big Blue Diamond in the company. That's the first time I'd ever heard that J-O-B stands for the Journey-Of-the-Broke."

"With my math background, I immediately saw the idea of geometric growth. I saw the idea of residual income and the distribution model. It actually looked darn good. That company had done about maybe $25 million in the previous year. I was pumped enough to look deeper."

"So, I talked to the owners, looked at their distribution strategy, product/marketing positioning, everything I'd learned at Harvard. I became convinced they would become a big, big, several hundred million dollar company. And with that I told Mary, 'Let's do it together.' And that's how we got started."

One thing that really hooked Warren on that first Saturday morning meeting was the statement: "In Network Marketing, you only succeed by helping other people succeed."

For Warren Nelson, corporate was, "Frankly dog-eat-dog. I knew full well that the corporate world is mostly politics and conformity. If you're entrepreneurial, you treasure freedom; you will really have a hard time being there. You also have a hard time helping people that work for you or who you work with do really well, because they'll use that to their advantage and you'll lose out in the end. It's a zero-sum game."

"So I loved the model of win-win, helping other people," Warren said. "I just was on fire when I saw the freedom, the ability to go fast, work with who you wanted to. And with my MBA background, I was really confidant that little company was going to turn out to be something big."

"It was an adventure," Warren said. "Imagine you are allowed to pick out a dozen of your best friends, the people most exciting, uplifting, inspiring, in your life and say, 'Hey, let's go on this wonderful adventure.' And you go out and just have great time and you all receive large financial rewards from it. That's fabulous."

"That's what it was like. It was like the greatest fantasy adventure that one could ever have in a lifetime. And learning from seven upline near-savants; every one of them was a million-dollar earner, all were brilliant at Network Marketing: Bill Hyman and Kay Smith, Jerry Campisi, Richard Kall, Craig Bryson and Craig Tillotson and Clara McDermott. Not recognition-driven type people: Giants of training, how-to and production. Good cheer, good humor, incredible work ethics, and in those three years I learned pretty much all the natural laws and principles of this business."

Warren went full-time in Network Marketing in January 1990, and for that he has to thank his wife, Mary.

"I was running an electronics company at the time, I had a very strong income, we had two young kids, and Mary said, 'Resign and do Network Marketing full-time.' She had no qualms, no doubts. Probably not many wives would do that, but Mary is courageous; she's a risk-taker, she's optimistic and she sees the upside of things. I went forward with her full support and confidence and we worked that business together."

"It was pretty much Mary built half and I built half," Warren said. "We worked a lot of in-home meetings, sometimes seven nights a week, two on Saturday. Tuesday night we did the tele-meetings for everybody in the Chicago area, whether they were downline or crossline or anybody. They all came, we did 'Super Saturdays.' It was just a phenomenal adventure."

"So, during the first three years," Warren said, "I developed the 'why' that really propelled me for the next 17-18 years:"

"The adventure, the freedom, the people, the lifestyle. It's been a joy. Every day I wake up and feel like clicking my heels.

I just love this business."

"Here's a great thing I learned in the beginning," Warren says. "It's easier to build it fast. Go as fast as you can for a year or a few years."

"And I mean fast both in terms of numbers of people you talk to and the hours you work," Warren said. "You're going to put more hours into it to start, so work at it more then and get it going fast."

"You think of it like a snowball," he said. "You roll it a little bit and it stops. You've got to keep rolling it, rolling it, rolling it till it gets bigger and bigger and bigger. Now it's starting to roll down the hill and it picks up size, and it gets as big as a house and you can't stop it if you wanted to. But if you don't push it fast enough, it doesn't get big fast enough to start rolling on its own."

"The sooner you do that the sooner you get positive reinforcement," Warren said. "The sooner you feel a little sense of, 'I'm getting somewhere,' some accomplishment and pride. All of us who have built to the top level, maybe we don't convey the fact that in the beginning we might have gotten discouraged if we hadn't gotten those little successes along the way."

"I was willing to persevere long and hard, even if I hit a flat spot and got disheartened," Warren said, "because I had enough successes. I feel a lot better when I get successes and if you build it faster you simply increase your odds of getting successes and more of them, too. That feeds you."

"Success begets success. When you

build fast, you have more success faster."

"And yet a person can only run a 100-yard dash for so many years before you kick back a little bit and take some deep breaths," Warren said. "I can never stay away from this business for too long. It's not my job. It's my passion. It's a lifestyle."

"When you do something you have passion for," Warren said, "it inspires you and propels you forward. And then you begin thinking of the excitement of other people who can get that adventure, freedom, that lifestyle, too. They can develop some financial independence," he says. "So they can begin to live where and how they like to live, and you care about them."

"I mean, the people in this business, they're just people that I deeply care about so much. I want them to be successful. And I mentor them; I talk to many of them every day, frequently, more than once a day. And it's the commitment to friends, loved ones that become like family over a period of time."

"And a family business it is," Warren adds, "with our daughter Beth Nelson Allen building her own successful Networking business with today's technology. What a joy!"

"It's excitement, it's adventure, and it's satisfying...

"...and it's inspiring because of the people that Mary and I help and serve."

"And I know a lot of people hear that but, but when you really get that lift from serving somebody... to my mind one of the greatest missions anyone can have is to start with the words 'to serve.'

Creating a Habit of Success

Linda Proctor was born in Columbus, Georgia. Her dad was in the military and when she was seven, they moved to Pensacola, Florida. It was, Linda says, a great place to grow up.

Pensacola is a small city, a busy seaport connected to the Gulf of Mexico and it is home to the United States Naval Air Station. That afforded Linda the opportunity to meet and make friends from all over North America and the world.

Linda says her family life was really like "Ozzie and Harriet," the 1950's television staple of the well-adjusted, idyllic American family. Linda had a great upbringing. Her family was very supportive and she felt secure and very, very protected.

Linda enjoyed being competitive and was always involved in sports. She did well academically, too, and went on to university, where she met Jack, her future husband. They got married and three years into the marriage, he passed away.

Linda's short married life was a mirror image of her family life. She was very protected by her husband and felt comfortable and secure. Her mother had passed away three months before her husband died; both from cancer. So, at the "ripe old age" of 23, Linda found herself a widow, alone and on her own. She had no support system. The umbrella of safety and security she had known all her life was gone.

She realized that it was up to her. Linda had to choose between cutting way back on her standard of living to suit her single paycheck as an accountant, or move forward and try to increase her income so she could support herself the way she really wanted to be living.

Linda made the decision to get into straight commission sales.

It was not an easy transition. Every time Linda took an aptitude test, she was told that she'd never make it in sales.

That was obviously discouraging, but Linda was convinced and committed to sales as the only way she was going to be able to increase her income. She persisted in securing a sales career and finally got a job selling life insurance. She was thrilled.

Linda went to her friends and family and told them her good news, but none of them shared her happiness. They saw themselves as targets for her sales efforts, and they let Linda know right away they had no intentions of buying life insurance from her. Their nay saying didn't dissuade Linda. She knew this was the path for her.

Four years into her sales career, Linda met the man who would become her mentor and husband, Bob Proctor, at a seminar he was doing for her company in Atlanta. Bob stood in the front of the room and asked, "Can you see yourself earning $100,000 a year?"

At that time (in the 1970s) Linda was struggling. She was earning $24,000 a year, working really hard. She was cold calling 200 people a week, getting 10 appointments and making one sale every three weeks. Her numbers were horrible. So, when Bob asked if she could see herself earning four times her current income, Linda figured she'd need to quadruple her efforts.

"Can I cold call 800 people a week?" Linda asked herself. And even if she could, did she want to?

Bob sat down with her and pointed out that to be successful you needed to know two things: Where you are and where you're going. He said, "There's no way doing what you're doing now you're going to reach the objectives you're setting." Bob told Linda, "You're going to have to work differently if you really want to move forward."

Bob made two simple suggestions: Be in front of someone every morning by 9:00, and ask everyone to buy $100,000 worth of life insurance? Linda agreed that she would.

Following Bob's counsel, Linda's results changed dramatically. Instead of making one sale every three weeks, she made 118 sales that year and earned a little less than half a million dollars. Lessons very well learned.

"It's about working smarter," Linda said. "And you don't have to believe in yourself to be able to achieve bigger results. When I started, I didn't believe in me. I believed in Bob and what he suggested I do. I just believed in Bob until I was able to believe in myself."

Linda performed at that level for a number of years, then, at Bob's suggestion, she started her own financial services company. Linda thought it was a great idea. Initially the business took off and all was right with the world, but over time, the overhead, managing employees, bringing in all the clients, the 70, 80, 90(!) hour weeks, wore Linda down to a frazzle.

One day, totally overwhelmed and feeling very sorry for her self, Linda went home early and crawled into bed. She literally pulled the covers over her head thinking, "I can't do this anymore." What she really wanted was for Bob to take over the business.

Bob came home a number of hours later and found Linda under the covers. "What are you doing?" he said. "What's wrong? Sit up here and talk to me." Linda never told him, "I want you to do it." She was hoping he'd get the message, but if anybody knows Bob, that's not what he was going to do.

Linda remembers him saying "I love you, and you have two options: "

> **"You can quit and I'll support you. Or I will mentor and coach you to do what needs to be done, but I will not do it for you."**

Although Linda was really ticked off with him for saying that, she knew he was right. And as it turns out, that's what led Linda to her extraordinary career in Network Marketing.

Bob was doing a speaking engagement in Barcelona and his host had provided two first-class tickets. He asked Linda if she wanted to go. Linda hadn't done much traveling at that point and would have loved to, but... she had her business to run. She couldn't.

Bob quoted Michael Gerber to her, "If your business requires your presence, you don't have a business. You have a job." Linda knew that's just what she had. She told Bob, "You know, I love working, I love having a career, but I really need to have it on my terms." Bob told her to write down her "terms."

Linda thought of a lot of things. At the top of her list of wants were: High income potential. A great product or service that offered real value. To work with interesting people all over the world. Good training and support (if she were going into something different). And above all, time freedom. She couldn't think of anything that provided all of that.

Bob could. He said, "What you've described is Network Marketing." Linda was not excited about that suggestion at all. She'd heard about all the failures in the business and remembers thinking, "I'm not going to argue. I'm just going to keep quiet and maybe he'll forget that suggestion."

But Bob countered, "Before you totally disregard the idea, I suggest that you talk to some people who've been successful in Network Marketing and then make your decision." Linda agreed and Bob introduced her to people who were earning the kind of money she wanted to earn.

"When I got in front of them, I realized I couldn't have been more wrong about this industry," Linda said. "The people who were making the larger incomes were doing it differently. I got very excited because I realized it was something that was in agreement with what I wanted to do, with my life purpose."

"To lead others to entrepreneurial situations that will reward them with time and money freedom."

Linda did very well. She earned six figures in her first year. In her second year it went to a quarter of a million. By her third year, it was over a half a million. Linda earned millions in her 12 years with that company.

Linda asked the people who became her upline mentors, "What does it look like to earn $100,000 a year?" They said, "Help six people earn $2,000 a month." Then Linda asked, "What does it look like to earn $1 million a year?" And they said, "Help six people earn $100,000 a year."

Linda knew that her goal was to be earning $1 million a year, so she set out to find a team of people that each wanted to earn $100,000 a year. Her approach was very direct. She'd say, "If I could show you how to earn an additional $100,000 a year doing something that I think you're going to find pretty interesting, perhaps different than what you think it is; working with a good solid team of people who know what they're doing would you sit down and have a coffee with me?"

Occasionally someone would ask, "What are you earning?" And Linda would say, "Well, I've just started, but the people who are mentoring me are earning that kind of income and if they can earn it we can earn it."

Linda had a vision, a goal, and she focused on it like a laser.

She was willing and able not to let the bumps in the road dissuade her. She was persistent and she picked great mentors to learn from.

Her husband taught her how to think outside the box. "Bob always pluses everything," she said. "We were working on our goals for the coming year and Bob told me, 'Take that number and multiply it times 1,000.' And I remember thinking, 'How in the heck will I ever do that kind of volume?' He just said, 'Play with it. Visualize how you would be living, how you would be working, what your business would look like.' That really expanded my mind—and my business."

"Bob gave me belief in myself," Linda said. "Because I moved forward and started having success, I no longer had to rely on him to believe in me to get results. I started believing in my own ability. And now what I do in Network Marketing is provide that belief for others who want to follow in similar footsteps."

Linda believes that people leave tracks just like the little animals do in her backyard after a snowfall. Those tracks are our habitual behavior.

"Successful people are in the habit of helping people."

They're in the habit of helping other people feel good, look good and get good results. One of the things Linda looks for in the people she's going to work with is the kind of habits they have; that's how she can tell what their success is going to be like.

Linda creates an environment where people that want to change can make those changes in their habits and get better results.

She believes that one of the biggest benefits Network Marketing provides is that it opens people's minds. Being able to entertain living anywhere you'd like, travel the way you'd love to, drive the kind of car you want, put your children in the best schools... is outside the realm of most people's thinking, because they don't have the vehicle to give them the income and the freedom of choice.

"Network Marketing will absolutely give you that," Linda says. "A lot of people come into Network Marketing and they don't believe it's possible, but if they're around people who are making it happen, their mind opens up and they come to believe that, yes, I can do this."

Linda Proctor became involved in Network Marketing to be able to have a satisfying career where she could make a difference in other people's lives and enjoy time and money freedom doing what she wanted to do. After 15 years, she continues to achieve those same goals and is starting fresh with a new company.

"Even people who don't succeed or stay in Network Marketing, leave a better person for having been in this industry," Linda says. "And when they stay..."

Big Picture

Sarah Robbins grew up in Troy, Michigan, where she lived most of her childhood years up until high school when the family moved to the "teeny tiny" town of Shawano, Wisconsin (2,076 families in the 2000 census) north of Green Bay. It was culture shock for Sarah, going from Troy, where all the kids got a car at 16. She said to her mom, "Oh man, all these kids are going to be wearing OshKosh overalls."

She was "devastated." It was pretty disorienting for a teenage girl in the midst of high school. Sarah soon realized that in taking her away from everything she knew, it actually allowed her to start over without any history. It was very freeing for Sarah and she quickly got to know some great friends there.

When she graduated, Sarah went to a private college in Minneapolis, Minnesota. "Another freezing cold place," she said. Sarah started her passion for teaching there.

During that time her family moved back to Michigan. Sarah missed them and wanted to be around them. So she moved back to Michigan. She got her degree and started teaching there. "Out in the cold again." Sarah has always been "really, *really,* ready to live somewhere warm."

> **"I was teaching kindergarten and first grade," Sarah said, "and that truly was my passion. I loved what I did."**

"Sometimes when I tell people that they laugh and say, 'You're surrounded by six-year-olds all day and you loved it?' Yeah, I did."

"I felt like it was what I was meant to do. And unfortunately," Sarah says, "because of Michigan's economy, I was facing losing my job. I had to pursue earning extra income somehow. We were in a tough place financially. That's why I started working for the high-end department stores. I was just kind of traveling around; doing events and demonstrations for different skin-care cosmetics lines."

One of the lines had first started in the up-scale department stores, which is where Sarah found it. The company became the number one clinical line in Nordstrom's. Sarah and her mother were both working for them as product educators. That was a way to bring in extra income alongside Sarah's full-time teaching job.

The company was looking for ways to bring dermatology to the masses. "They felt this line wasn't best kept under glass," Sarah said. "But the doctors who own the company, being two of the world's most successful dermatologists and entrepreneurs, also wanted to empower other people to do what they've done. Long story short, we got a call from them that would change our lives."

"They were going to be leaving retailing after being very successful and get into Network Marketing," she said. "This was their first time doing that." And what a smart move that turned out to be. Today Sarah's organization alone brings in more volume than Nordstrom's ever did.

Last year she earned a very high six-figure income. One month, her commission check, with bonuses totaled over six figures. This will be her first millionaire year.

Sarah Robbins has been in Network Marketing for two years. She's 28 years old.

"It's really exciting at my age," Sarah says, "to truly have found something that has been so life-changing for me and my family."

And "exciting" was not what Sarah thought when she first heard about the opportunity.

"My previous history in Network Marketing was short, not sweet," Sarah said. "A friend signed me up and nobody talked to me again after that. I left as quickly as I came in. So the only thing I knew about it was that I would never ever, ever, ever, do it!"

"I'll never forget when I heard about this," Sarah said. "My mom said, 'Sarah, I know the stories of people who start in the beginning and they work the business. We've got the brand recognition. We've got the market and economic timing and we're doing this.' And I'm like, Hmm… I don't know about *that.*"

But then Sarah talked to her friend Doug Firebaugh. Doug does a lot of training in the industry and he was a very successful leader in his company. Sarah and her husband attended a Bible study group with Doug. They sat down together and asked, "What do you think?"

"I'll never forget him just staring right at me from across the table and saying, 'You have no clue what you found do you?' I just smiled politely and he said, 'To find something with this name recognition and this timing... These opportunities come once every couple of decades. Quit over-thinking this and start telling people about it today!'"

Her mom had said it. An industry expert confirmed it. Fear of loss set in on Sarah immediately.

She thought, "If my mom does this and I don't, but I knew I had the opportunity, I'm going to regret it." And her urgent needs came in, too. "I'm going to lose my job. I'm going to lose my home. We have a lot of debt." And Sarah was thinking, "Do I really have another option? Do I have another way or am I going to continually be in the squeal?"

She decided to get started. "I'll never forget my husband telling me, 'Sarah, you know this is a great company and you know you're a hard worker and you don't quit,' and I remember thinking, 'If I could retire in 10 years from teaching, that would be great. Then I'll be able to put my time and energy into my family, my own children.'"

Sarah had absolutely no clue how it was going to go and grow. When she got started there were a handful of people in the corporate office, a couple of them being her own age, no trainers; not even any training material. Everybody was looking at each other, going, "What's next?" They didn't have any maps. They were pioneers.

Sarah says she started by failing forward. "But we all know," she says, "success is just getting up more often than you fall down."

Since, Sarah didn't have anybody to follow and tell her what to do, she fell down right away. Her mom said, "This is huge. Don't tell anybody else about this opportunity." So at first the two of them were only selling products. They were making a couple thousand dollars a month and were happy about that, especially Sarah on her teacher's salary.

Sarah started researching the industry. As a teacher, she was always studying and learning new things. So she bought some books and CDs. She grabbed onto *Networking Times,* which she loved, and read every page, highlighting, making notes. Sarah at once realized the power and purpose of leverage—and that changed everything. "Let's start telling everybody about the opportunity," she said, and she did.

"The creators of the most successful acne solution in history just went into Network Marketing," she would tell people. "This is ground-floor. This is going to be huge. Invite everybody. We've got a meeting going on. Bring an armful of people. This is going to blow your mind." They had 300 people in their very first meeting.

Little did Sarah know she was already teaching people how to duplicate her success.

"Tell people this, share and invite, bring them to the meeting, ask them to join you" and it worked.

When her people ask Sarah, "What do you talk about when you tell people about our opportunity?" She tells them, "The four P's: Talk about the Products. Talk about the Partnership we have with the doctors. Talk about the Pay-plan. And talk about the Positioning, the timing that they have to be in at the beginning, and for them to expand as we expand across the nation and then internationally."

One of Sarah's defining moments in this business came was when she was earning about a couple thousand dollars just selling products. She was having a very hard time recruiting. There was a woman who had found an online ad for the company and she called Sarah, and talked to her about the opportunity. Her husband was a former member of the New York Stock Exchange. He'd gone online looking for an opportunity for his wife. He called her and said, "This is an amazing business opportunity. You're doing this." He said, "Tell everybody you know, all your friends, and in six months your residual income will be insane."

So she called Sarah and asked her about everything and said, "What are you doing tonight?" Sarah said, "I'm doing an event in Ohio." The woman drove eight hours and showed up at the end of the event, put the products on her hand, and said, "Let's go out to eat."

They sat down and she said to Sarah, "I'm ready to get started now." Sarah said, "Look, I'm really tired. Let's do this tomorrow." She now knows what a foolish and risky thing that was to say, and thanks God the woman was still excited and that she signed up the next day.

In six months that woman developed an ongoing six-figure, residual income from her efforts. Sarah's check tripled in one month and she said, "Okay, this works." From then on, "It was amazing."

Sarah had a massive organization starting to build, and her confidence just went through the roof.

Sarah jokes that before that time, she was the least-highest income earner in the company. Today, she is #1.

"I believe very strongly in sowing back into people," Sarah says. "It's that idea of reciprocity, and really, you get what you give. The company just announced a new enhancement to our compensation plan giving an extra percentage on bottom generations. It can add significantly to your income. I've already qualified for them all."

"So, I decided to reinvest that money back into my leaders," Sarah said. "The way I look at it that was income I didn't have before. They're the ones helping to qualify me, so I'm using the funds to reinvest back into them."

"Whether it's traveling to their market to help them grow, or challenges and incentives, or recognition, it's simply sowing back into my leaders. Because, really" Sarah says, "our greatest asset in this business is not products, no matter how great they are—and I'm not discounting our products ever. Our greatest asset is our team. I'm always teaching the importance of their speaking life and speaking truth and speaking positivity into their groups. Then we take that and we pass it on."

"It's also the importance of abundance and recognition and being the leader that they're looking for," Sarah said. "It's being those things to their team as well. You can definitely see how all of these things have translated down. We've truly got an amazing group of leaders."

"It is all about what I can do to really change other people's lives."

"I tell people, 'My check will grow every month now that we've experienced this exponential growth and we're getting the duplication and all of this excitement and momentum. My check grows every month regardless of what I do now."

"Quite frankly," she says. "I could stop today and be happy with the income that's growing and that's already there, but I'm working just as diligently now as I did in the beginning, because for me, it's 'big picture.' I want to fund my own foundation for women and children through my Network Marketing business. Today I am fortunate to *give* more than I used to *earn.*"

"I mean, this is what drives me, it's what fuels me, it's what makes me happy. It makes me excited just to see other people's lives change. So I just have 'big picture,' and I feel like I haven't even begun yet. That's really what keeps me going and moving and growing."

"It's not tangible things; not cars and homes. I'll get those. I'll even finally get to live someplace warm, so I'm good with all that," Sarah says. "For me, the paychecks are numbers, but the *experiences* and the way you can change people's lives is what's most important."

"I know Donna Johnson, she's a mentor of mine and she's created so many millionaires in her organization. I want to see the same thing happen with our group. I want to help them all really achieve their dreams."

Seeds of Greatness

Finn Ørjan Saele grew up outside of Bergen, the second largest city in Norway. He was the second child. His mother was a parliament member in Norway for 12 years. His dad was the editor of a newspaper. "When I was growing up I got a really good family with a fantastic mom and a fantastic dad," Ørjan says.

He describes life in his school years as "quite, quite good," which is surprising, because Ørjan faced a couple of daunting obstacles. "My problem was I was dyslexic," he said. "That was discovered when I was in seventh grade. Before that I was just a kid that couldn't read and write, and of course that colors you, because you feel stupid—and other people think you're stupid."

In his first years of school, the other kids liked to tease Ørjan, because he was a very skinny little boy, easy to push around. And since he was different, having special reading and language classes the other children didn't attend, he became the victim of kids that wanted to bully him.

All of that changed in high school. Ørjan not only went to a new school, he got bigger and all of sudden grew muscles. Now he could defend himself. Ørjan also did Thai boxing for a couple of years. After that, nobody bullied him anymore.

He joined Network Marketing while in his last year of high school.

Ørjan's uncle, who is five years older than he is, got him involved in a weight loss company. It was just before his 18th birthday, and the company wasn't opened in Norway yet.

"I was incredibly skeptical after the first meeting," Ørjan said. "I was sure this could not be right. I didn't know if it was a pyramid scheme, if it was just a scam, but I was sure they didn't tell me the whole truth. Actually one of the reasons I joined was to prove to my uncle it was wrong."

Ørjan had seen this Swedish guy draw the circles on the board and he did the math. The way it was presented, the company would easily pay out several hundred percent. Ørjan sat down for about three weeks and took apart the compensation plan, studying the different rules, looking for where the breaks were.

He concluded that, in fact, they probably didn't pay out too much money, but he had to join to see for himself what they actually did pay, and to learn if this really was a legitimate business.

His uncle continued to tell him about new Network Marketing opportunities, and every time he showed Ørjan something, he let him know he could become a millionaire overnight. At that, Ørjan would argue, argue and argue. He knew that couldn't be possible.

"Business is not that easy."

"In the process," Ørjan said, "I realized the system was true, and if you spent time on it, you had one benefit which you didn't have with a regular job: There was no cap on your income. However," he added, "your income in the beginning of the business would be less—a lot less—than if you spent the same time on a regular job."

No limit on your income impressed Ørjan greatly. He saw how, if you just continued working, you could make twice as much, or three times as much, or 10 times as much as in a job. That intrigued him enough to do the business—and that's the reason why he didn't give up. This is important, because in the beginning Ørjan didn't do well at all.

"I did as bad as you can do," Ørjan says, laughing. "The first business was weight loss and consumables, and I did get some people involved. But before I actually managed to put them into the computer and get the products to Norway, I was stopped dead. I got three pages in the local Bergen newspaper—because of my mom's and dad's notability—saying that this was probably illegal and that the products would cause cancer."

"The shampoo would cause cancer if you ate it, was basically the headline and the content of the article. I would ask people, 'You don't eat shampoo, do you?' But my dad and my mom and I got the front page. The newspaper ended my career in that company."

Ørjan joined an environmental cleaning company, where he cleaned a lot of cars and lots of windows. He was 19, and that's where he built his first real downline. Ørjan made a lot of money from retail sales, but in two years, only $300 in actual commissions from his team.

But when Ørjan got that check he was on fire!

He was jumping and running around in the living room of his mom's and dad's house for about five minutes straight! He was so excited his sister thought he'd won the lottery, but he told her, "No, no, no, this is much better. The circles work."

Ørjan soon joined the first of the U.S. telecoms to come to Norway, and the first company to really pay him. After four years in the business, he had only made about $350 or $400, and was at the $100-a-month level.

"When you believe in a certain way, you think in a certain way, which will cause you to act in a certain way," Ørjan says. Now he believed. And he was ready to build his biggest team so far.

Even though they didn't understand how things really worked, Ørjan and his people were just so excited. "We believed we'd get rich really quickly," he says. "Once all of us owned that belief, we started thinking and acting that way: We had urgency. We couldn't wait. We had to do it now, as fast as possible."

That urgency caused Ørjan and his entire team to take massive action. They started putting in 80-90 hours a-week, traveling all over Norway building the presentations, and the meetings, and selling the product.

"We got tremendous growth," Ørjan said, "and after about three weeks in that company, my check was about $1,800-1,900 a week. It was about $10,000 a month from the second month." How did *that* happen?

"I believe that if you do something and you work hard on it, eventually through a whole lot of Plan, Do, Check and Adjust, you'll find a way that works," he says. "We built the business in the beginning even though we didn't have the knowledge. We just did whatever other people in that company were doing, and tried to do it better."

Ørjan went on the MLM cruise and got to know Tom "Big Al" Schreiter, met Art Jonak and Michael Clouse. He hooked up with Randy Gage in South Beach and went to his MLM Power Weekend in Orlando. All of that brought new ideas of how to do the business on a more professional level. He went back home and together with his team created a system that worked.

Ørjan says there are five behaviors that you need to have down to succeed in Network Marketing.

"Number one behavior is developing a big smile."

The second behavior is that *each one will reach one,* so you've got to learn how to contact and invite people.

Third is *each one teach one.* "You got to have a system for duplication, because you will never make a million dollars in Network Marketing unless you get duplication. Without duplication," Ørjan says, "you should go get a job. It will serve you much better." You teach people to bring people into the system and you teach people to become speakers, trainers and teachers.

Number four is *connecting people.* "I think that it's crucial that you become a networker," Ørjan says. "Too many Network Marketers aren't networkers after they join the business. Connecting people is making sure all the new people on your team are connected to several people in their upline. That's how leaders are developed."

"If you have a brand new person in the business," Ørjan says, "and they signed up two people, and their sponsor has been in for three days, and that's all the people this new person knows. He knows four people that never made a dime in Network Marketing."

"When you connect him with five, six or seven upline leaders, he knows four or five of them who are making full-time incomes. Some of them may be making $100,000 a month. That's the importance of networking inside of Networking."

Number five is *becoming teachable.* "You have to get into the growth process," Ørjan says, "so you're doing the personal development as well as the skills of Network Marketing.

"Being teachable means you learn something and you implement that," Ørjan says. "Being teachable is not just reading the books, going to the events, listening to the CDs. It's putting that new knowledge to work in your life."

"If you implement those five behaviors in a step-by-step training system," Ørjan says, "there is nothing that can stop anybody from making it to the top of any Network Marketing company in the world. That's all it takes. If you keep doing them you will become better at some of the skills and eventually you find one or two or three where you're world-class—and then you'll be paid world-class money."

Ørjan stresses the importance of your "why," the dream, because his "why" was and is so important to him.

"In the beginning, I wanted to make money," he says, "At least $10,000 a month, because that would give me my dream lifestyle. My 'why' wasn't really the money, it was the dream lifestyle. $10,000 a month when you're 17 will give you that lifestyle. And then I kept increasing the amount, so that it could cover my growing lifestyle dreams."

"When you become a multi-millionaire and you don't have to go out and work to make money, new 'whys' appear. Today, one of my 'whys' is mastery—wanting to be the best of who I can be in my field."

"When you fulfill so many of your dreams in our business, a big 'why' develops in that you want to help other people achieve what you have achieved. You want to show other people the way they can do the same thing that you've mastered yourself."

"I still have a money amount that I'm always working toward," Ørjan says, "but my wife Hilde and I have a vision of helping a million kids out of poverty. And not only out of poverty: The dream is to develop the kids into leaders that could be leading companies in a third world nation 30-40 years from now. It's a dream about all the people you can help to develop into their potential. I think that happens in Network Marketing more and faster than in most other businesses. I get a lot of excitement out of seeing people's potential."

"Your dream has to be so big and so real that it's worth it and you're willing to delay your gratification and you'll take the time to do everything that is necessary to reach that dream."

> **"I believe that people have seeds of greatness inside of them, and I would love to live a life where I could get those seeds growing on the inside of more and more people."**

That's Ørjan's vision for his life: Kids that are brought out of poverty, adults finding their dream again. He believes that by growing those seeds you will grow to become a great person. "And when more people become a great person," he says, "they will in their turn discover more seeds inside of more people and eventually we will be living in a great world."

Ørjan has a favorite quote by Phillips Brooks: "Be such a man, and live such a life, that if every man were such as you, and every life a life like yours, this earth would be God's Paradise."

"I think our greatest fear," Ørjan says, "should not be that we won't succeed, but that we will succeed at something that doesn't matter. And as you can see, Network Marketing really matters."

Who Leads the Leaders?

Carolyn Wightman says she grew up as plain vanilla. "I was just basic. I didn't come from a broken family. I certainly did not have a silver spoon in my mouth. I mean, I wore hand-me-down clothes and that sort of thing, but nobody was ever starving."

Carolyn was born and raised in and around Washington D.C. The house that they lived in was right across the river in Virginia, and when the trees were trimmed, Carolyn would look out her window on a view of the nation's Capitol and the Washington Monument.

Carolyn remembers her father taking her to an Inauguration Day parade, sitting on his shoulders looking up at the White House on Pennsylvania Avenue. She sensed the history all around her and Carolyn felt she was somehow part of it.

Her family moved from D.C. and she went to high school in Illinois. When it was time for college, Carolyn's parents said, "Don't look at where the college is and whether you can get a scholarship or not. Let's just make the decision and then we'll figure it out." Carolyn decided she was going west. She was able to get "a very expensive" Liberal Arts degree and somehow, it did get *figured out.*

At the time, California seemed like it was off the planet because it was so very far away. Things like long distance calls were really *long distance.* It took days to drive back and forth, and most people never had the money to fly.

Carolyn loved the idea that where she went to school was near the mountains, *and* near the ocean, *and* had the fabulous city of San Francisco around it.

"There was such enormous variety and versatility, and a sort of open-mindedness that was very energizing."

In the middle of her college career, Carolyn made a deal with her parents that if they would give her the tuition for two semesters, she would go live in Italy as long she could afford to. That was in the days of "Europe-on-$5-a-Day," and she did even better than that. Carolyn stayed for eight months.

The first thing she did when she returned to the States was to take a summer internship back in Washington. She was assigned to the office of a Congressman. They were short on staff, so Carolyn ended up with way more responsibility than a college intern normally was given. As a result of her efforts, the Congressman asked her to come and work, "as his congressional staff in the district" in the fall, which just happened to be in California where her parents had recently moved.

From all her experiences Carolyn discovered that she had a real curiosity and passion for the political process.

"I was especially fascinated with decision-making and leadership."

Carolyn married and she and her husband pioneered the first Peace Corps program in Polynesia. They were there for three years, returning to the States in 1969 and ended up in Southern California.

It was time for Carolyn to find work.

She had her experience in Washington, her Liberal Arts degree, she spoke a Polynesian language... what else? Nothing had prepared her for anything except getting more education and teaching—and she just couldn't see herself in front of a classroom.

Get a job? Working for somebody, commuting in traffic every morning, getting home really late, working the day after Christmas. If someone comes in from out of town, you can't take time off to be with them and make it up later. None of that appealed to her at all.

Carolyn was home with her family for Thanksgiving and, dutiful daughter that she was, helped her mom with the dishes and laundry. Her mother kept telling her, "Don't use very much of this now. It's really concentrated, just a little tiny bit—and it doesn't pollute."

In Polynesia, everything was pure and crystal clear. In Southern California, you couldn't breathe the air and you shouldn't drink the water. That contrast was alarming for Carolyn even before the words "biodegradable, environmental, ecology" came into people's vocabulary—and true to her Peace Corps roots—Carolyn was looking for a way she could be part of the solution, instead of the problem.

She asked her mom, "Where do you get this stuff?" Her mother said, "I don't know. I think it's one of those door-to-door businesses, and you've got to wait until someone knocks on your door."

Carolyn lived 400 miles away from her mother's door, so that wasn't very helpful. Carolyn called the company and asked, "Where can I buy this stuff?" They connected her with someone who was nearby.

A woman came over to Carolyn's house, dropped off a "confidential price list" saying, "...and maybe you'd like to be a distributor." Carolyn told her, "I'm not interested in selling anything. All I want to do is buy these products." The woman took Carolyn to the home of her sponsors.

"I had the sense that anyone who did this probably lived in a trailer park," Carolyn says. "Probably had a rabid dog that was tied to a tree with a chain, and a couple of cars in the yard up on cinderblocks with bald tires." That's honestly what she thought.

"Who else would be in a door-to-door business except somebody who is really down and out?"

Instead, Carolyn was taken to a lovely home in Beverly Hills—the *real* Beverly Hills with movie stars up and down the street. The house was beautiful with a three-car garage that had an apartment above it where the Japanese housekeeper who helped raise the family's four children lived. Both the husband and the wife were stockbrokers. Their home office was in their oldest son's room. He was off at Harvard Law School. "This does not exactly fit the picture I was expecting," Carolyn thought.

"In this business, we think you have to be clever and be a really good salesperson," Carolyn says. "And you have to have a good presentation and be really persuasive. But their housekeeper spoke very broken English. She offered me a protein drink in a little crystal glass on a silver tray. I told her no, thank you very much, I just wanted the cleaning products. She looked at me and said, 'You feel good now. You use this, you feel better. You try.'"

"That's how I got in the business, and that was four decades ago"

In the beginning, Carolyn used a few products, gave some more away as Christmas presents, but that was pretty much it. Then her sponsors invited her to a meeting. Carolyn didn't want to go, but did so as a courtesy. All the while wondering, "What am I doing here?"

The man presenting the meeting talked about what the business was like for him. All Carolyn heard was he'd just gotten a new car.

He and his family had just earned some exotic trip to somewhere. He had just made $2,000 in that past month... *That* got her attention. $2,000 back then was *a lot* of money to Carolyn.

"Frankly, he wasn't particularly inspiring," Carolyn remembers. "I looked at him and thought, 'If that guy can do it, I ought to be able to do half that—and it certainly beats working for the phone company. Maybe I ought to give this a shot.' That's how I *backed* into the business."

Carolyn had no idea what she was doing. Her mentors gradually brought her along, "on their apron strings," she says.

This was 40 years ago. There was no Internet, no conference or three-way calling. Long distance phone calls were too expensive to make during the day, so Carolyn only made calls after 11 at night when the rates went down. Occasionally someone would record a cassette tape and she'd share that with people.

So Carolyn built her business sharing stories and through word of mouth. She didn't have a map or a model. People asked her how to do the business and she'd say, "I don't know. Just find something you're enthusiastic or passionate about and tell people."

One sale at a time... One new business partner at a time... Over time, Carolyn watched her business ever-so-slowly grow.

"The thing I did best,' she says, "is I didn't quit."

Carolyn was never motivated by money. Her purpose in the business was really to connect with people and give them some choices in their lives.

She did realize that money may a big motivator for some people, and since you couldn't make money in her business without having products that would make you healthier, and support the planet, and get some of the toxins out of your life, Carolyn's mission was going to be accomplished, regardless. That's what was really important to her. Still is.

Carolyn always makes sure that the objectives people are looking for fit and match what it is that she has to offer. If she has to tweak some things to make it work for them, she can do that.

Carolyn stopped trying to fit square pegs into round holes long ago. She's certain that the approach of, "This is the way it is, do this and that and this," is a very limiting way to do business and simply doesn't work. Carolyn focuses on finding the win-win. Even more, she's out to create win-times-win. Win^2.

The kinds of people Carolyn finds most attractive and are the most successful, are people who see themselves as leaders. Leaders are willing to take responsibility for their behavior and also for their results. Leaders are people who are not blaming someone else or some other circumstance for what it is they do. Leaders are looking for a challenge that allows them to live in integrity with their life and values, and also to be rewarded for that as richly as they choose.

Carolyn always looks to see who leads the leaders.

"It's all about Possibilities," Carolyn says. "I go back to my old Peace Corps roots: If you're not part of the solution, you're part of the problem."

"There are so many problems out there that anyone can see, whether it has to do with our life or economics or finances or how we deal with our children or health or all of these things. I think that it's easy to get on a bandwagon and go, 'Oh, I don't like this,' and 'Oh, I wish that had happened,' or go out and take a flag and march down the street for some cause. That by itself does not create solutions."

"What I love most about Network Marketing and my business is that I can stay committed to possibilities; possibilities for financial education, possibilities for being able to live a life with vitality and energy."

"It's being able to see solutions and not just problems."

"To actually have something that if people are in a conversation about, 'Oh, I don't feel good, Oh, this doesn't work. Oh...' whatever it is, to know that I actually have a choice I might be able to offer them."

That doesn't mean that Carolyn has the only choice, and it doesn't mean that others have to do it her way.

"To be able to offer someone the possibility of a solution and not just living in a problem, I find very emancipating—for both of us," she says.

"That provides an inspiration for people. If they like living being unhappy, then God bless them. That's fine. But if they want to do something else, let's keep exploring some ways that Network Marketing can make that happen."

Afterword

Each of the Network Marketers in this book became successful—very successful... millionaires.

There are many thousands just like them in this business all around the world.

Most of the people who read this book will not become millionaires.

But some of you... the ones that read the book again and again... those who read until the stories become part of you... you *will* begin to think and feel and act like *The Greatest Networkers in the World.*

Remember their clear message:

"If we can do it, so can you."

That's the good news.

The bad news is: Now you have no more excuses.

It will take time. It will take effort. You have to learn the skills. You have to work on yourself. And you cannot quit. But do those things and you will become successful—perhaps very successful, maybe even a millionaire.

Network Marketing will transform your life.

Let me know what I can do to help.

Thanks

In the development of this book project there're many people to whom I am most grateful.

They include:

The men and women in the book—without them this wouldn't have happened.

Richard Brooke for suggesting the idea to me.

Unnamed others for their care and advice.

My wife and family for their love and support.

And GOD.

Thank you, all.

I appreciate you.

John Fogg

Since the late '80s I've been working in Network Marketing and personal growth & professional development as:

Author/co-author/editor of more than two-dozen well-known and some best-selling books, including *The Greatest Networker in the World*—which, having sold more than a million copies, is among the highest-ever selling Network Marketing titles and often considered to be the best known.

Founder/co-founder of several US-published business magazines including Upline, Network Marketing Lifestyles, Networking Times, and TheNetworkMarketingMagazine.com.

Coach and mentor to more-than-I-can-count individual Network Marketers.

My speaking appearances have taken me around the world.

I've been blessed to have been able to positively impact the lives of millions of people.

I live with my family in Virginia, USA.